TWO PIECES OF PAPER

TWO PIECES OF PAPER

Honest Advice for Getting a Degree and a Job in the Modern Working World

SKYLER W. KING

M·J

NEW YORK

LONDON • NASHVILLE • MELBOURNE • VANCOUVER

Two Pieces of Paper

Honest Advice for Getting a Degree and a Job in the Modern Working World

© 2020 Skyler W. King

Published in New York, New York, by Morgan James Publishing. Morgan James is a trademark of Morgan James, LLC. www.MorganJamesPublishing.com

ISBN 9781642798111 paperback
ISBN 9781642798128 eBook
Library of Congress Control Number: 2019914080

Cover & Interior Design by:
Christopher Kirk
www.GFSstudio.com

Morgan James is a proud partner of Habitat for Humanity Peninsula and Greater Williamsburg. Partners in building since 2006.

Get involved today! Visit
MorganJamesPublishing.com/giving-back

DEC 1 5 2020

Dedication

For Tegan
And everyone else trying to play their hand

Contents

Preface

I am a recent college graduate sharing advice with you on how to get a degree and a job by the end of your college experience. I am not a Human Resources expert, nor do I have any hiring experience. Frankly, I'm not entirely sure what I'm doing in life about half the time. That being said, it's a pretty safe bet that most adults are the same way. Unless you believe in reincarnation (which is totally cool if you do), everyone goes through the game of life once and only once. When we all ultimately die, nobody has more experience in living than anyone else. That's why I am confident in what I'm saying in this book. It's not because I have more than 30 years of experience hiring college graduates or developing careers, but because I feel like I've learned how to successfully get through school and get a job.

Also, this is a book of best practices. I can honestly say that I did not prescribe to everything in this book to the letter. I'm saying this because, for one, I hate hypocrites; and for me to feed you advice without admitting that I didn't eat all my own dog food would make me a hypocrite. I also think it's important to say I didn't follow everything in the book as a way to say that nobody is perfect. You could work your ass off and potentially get no job, or you could be a complete slacker and somehow get the job of your dreams. Is it fair? No, but life isn't. My hope is that you make your own luck with the help of this book. I can't guarantee you the job of your dreams, but I can guarantee that you'll be in a better position to graduate and get one than you would if you didn't read this book. Enjoy!

Acknowledgments

This project is something that I could definitely not do alone, and I am forever blessed to have had the pleasure of meeting such talented and helpful people this early in my life. First and foremost, I have to thank my experts for taking time out of their busy lives to support this effort and volunteer their insight and expertise. Beyond that, I have to thank them for their mentorship even before I had the idea of authoring this book. Your willingness to help me then and now speaks volumes of your character, and I hope to one day be as generous as you all.

I have to also thank my friends, John and Madelyn, who listened to one of my now infamous cigar talks and inspired me to believe that not only could I complete this work, but that it would also be beneficial. To everyone that read through early versions of the book and gave me their thoughts—in particular, my sister Maggie, my cousin Sarah, and friends, Erin, Nicole, Kingsley, and Mason—your words helped shape what lies in these pages today. I especially have to thank my brother Tegan for sitting with me and combing through the edited version as a member of my target audience and affirming that the book has value.

Speaking of editing, I would be remiss if I did not acknowledge the hard work of my editor, Kathie-Jo, who came as a saving grace for someone with no publishing experience. I am forever appreciative of your hard work in making this book the best version of itself. I also have to thank Sandra, my go-to graphic designer, for the amazing cover art.

I also thank you, the reader, for your support of this book. I hope this helps you in some way and that you disseminate the knowledge you obtain as much as possible to help others get their two pieces of paper.

Lastly, I have to thank both God and my family. If I lost everything, I know that I would have my family to fall back on, and the support my Mom and Dad have given me throughout my life made this project possible. God has blessed me, as he does everyone, with an incredible amount of talent. I am forever grateful I was able to channel that gift into a means to help young people everywhere succeed and hopefully carry out His will.

Introduction

Let me start off by saying, congratulations! You are about to enter—or are currently in—one of the most exciting times of your life: college. In college, you will have some of the most fun you will ever have in life. However, in addition to the loads of fun you plan to have, why are you going to college? Why have you decided to spend tens of thousands of dollars over the next 4, 5, or maybe even 6 years of your life? Why are you willing to accrue an amount of debt equal to what some people spend on a small house? For a piece of paper with your school's name in fancy letters above your name?

In his *Kid Gorgeous* special on Netflix®, comedian John Mulaney joked about the whopping cost of his English degree: "I paid $120,000 for someone to tell me to go read Jane Austen, and then I didn't." He recalled walking across a stage at graduation, hungover, in a gown, to accept a certificate for reading books that I didn't read. Strolling across a stage, the sun in my eyes, my family watching as I sweat vodka and ecstasy, to receive a 4-year degree in a language that I already spoke.

Most people go to college for the same reason as Mulaney, amassing all that debt just to get a certificate. They work hard for around half a decade only to work just as hard for the rest of their life.

You're going to college to ultimately get a good, well-paying job[1]. My hope is that by the end of this book, you will be in a better situation than John Mulaney was when he finished college. My hope for you is that you finish college not just with the debt you amassed and the degree you received, but also with a job offer in your back pocket that will allow you to both work off the debt and do something you love while being successful in your career.

Like Mulaney, I walked across the stage and got my certificate. No, I was not sweating vodka or ecstasy, and I was graduating in Cyber Engineering rather than English. But I had one more thing going for me: the comfort of having accepted an incredible job offer. Over the course of the following 3 years, that offer from a major telecommunications company would take me around the country and allow me to learn more about the different roles within my degree field. Using the same strategies I share in this book, many of my peers also left school with great job opportunities at companies such as Charles Schwab™, Dow® Chemical, Blue Origin™, Cisco®, International Paper™, Folgers®, Wal-Mart®, and Aldi®, among others.

While I was going through school, I was very fortunate to have the opportunities afforded to me. However, replicating an experience similar to mine is not out of the realm of possibility for any college student. I kept an academic focus and, ultimately, finished my degree program with honors. I was involved in extracurricular activities and held leadership positions in some. I had the respect of my peers, professors, and university administrators. I had several internships and an on-campus job working in a student lab facility. All of these things were possible for me, and I'm certain they are possible for you as well. In fact, you might exceed my accomplishments.

At the time of this writing, there is an economic boom. Employers are hiring more people than ever and offering great incentives to their new hires, such as higher wages, comfortable benefits packages, and flexible work lifestyles. You are very lucky to be beginning your college career now. By taking the initiative to read this book, whether you bought it on your own or it was given to you as a gift, you have taken the first step in setting yourself apart from your peers, who will also be looking for work. You will make the student debt crisis seem obsolete with your ability to repay your debts quickly, and perhaps TruTV will cancel the show *Paid Off*, which is designed to help struggling individuals pay off their debt. I'm not going to give you money to pay off your debt, but I will give you the tools you need to get out and succeed on your own.

The skills you will learn in this book apply to any person with the goal of getting a job right out of school, regardless of what university, college, community college, or technical school you attend. Whether you are studying liberal arts, business, applied sciences, or engineering, this book has the strategies you need to set yourself apart from your peers. Specifically, this book gives you advice on shaping your college career (or whatever is left of it) for getting that *other* piece of paper you are working toward at the same time: the job offer.

The foundation of higher education has shifted. The purpose of college is not just to gain greater knowledge in a certain discipline, but also to achieve a basic understanding and skills in a discipline before entering the workforce. College students of the next generation are looking for two things when they are finished with their schooling: a degree and an acceptable job offer. This is the mindset you must carry as you go through your college career: Get those two pieces of paper. A degree alone is not sufficient to get the job you want. Your degree might show you have the knowledge needed in your major, but that knowledge alone will not directly translate to a position in the workplace. Similarly, even if you have the work experience and connections sufficient to perform in the job of your dreams, your lack of a degree will likely prevent you from actually filling that role, or at least limit your advancement to future roles. These two pieces of paper (as I will often refer to them) will objectively change your life. They should be received at the same time and, to do that, you must work on them in parallel.

Let me be clear that this book is not a "get a job tomorrow" book. While this book does include things you can do today to improve your chances at employment, there is about equal content related to developing a successful collegiate lifestyle. If you think about it, it is far easier to develop habits in your younger years than later in your life; and building a strong foundation will propel you into success not just in college, but throughout your future career. By following the advice in this book, you will be in a position to succeed in getting the job you want and, ideally, not have to scramble to get yourself together after walking across the stage.

In this book, I've broken down what I've found to be the major factors of your college career related to receiving your two pieces of paper. First and foremost is your academic life, as it is the primary reason you are in school. Having academics as your bedrock will prove to be a sound foundation for your success. Aside from academic life, it is almost equally important to have a healthy life outside of school. Being involved allows you to explore your interests, to find out what you like and don't like, and ultimately to have fun while going through the rigors of higher education. Along with your participation in academic and extracurricular endeavors, you must also be able to effectively communicate what you do in those endeavors. You might be the most well-qualified candidate ever, but you won't land the job if you can't sell your skills. This practice in communicating effectively will help when searching for internships, cooperative education programs (co-op) experiences, and full-time offers, as well as ultimately securing those roles. Finding those opportunities can be tricky and landing them can be even more difficult without adequate preparation. Once you have that internship or co-op, doing well in that temporary role will be critical before entering into the full-time workforce, because that opportunity could potentially lead to an offer upon its completion.

Each chapter in this book outlines things that you can do to help yourself succeed, as well as ways to help yourself make those things a part of your regular life. Some points in the book will have a note entitled "Looking Ahead." These notes are to combat the possibility of your reading and thinking to yourself, "This is stupid. Why am I doing this?" I get that, and like you I hate doing something if I don't know *why* I'm doing it. So, if you're ever thinking, "What's the point of this?" then I'd encourage you to look for a Looking Ahead note.

At the end of each chapter is a section called "Ask the Experts," where working professionals in both industry and academia share their advice for success on the topic at hand. These individuals have extensive Human Resources or industry experience and have proven to be leaders in their disciplines through their own hard work and dedication. I've asked them to help with this book because they have as much desire as I do to assist you as you enter the workforce, and they were more than willing to help in any way they could.

College is an exciting time in your life, and the opportunities a successful college experience can give you are endless. You are investing a large amount of money for the years you spend in school; and I hope by the end of your college career, you will see a very clear return on your investment. So, without further delay, let's start working on your two pieces of paper.

Chapter 1

Academics: Getting What You Paid for

T he goal of this book is to get you your two pieces of paper—one of those being a college degree. While a college degree is no more than a certificate from your school that certifies you as capable of a higher level of thought in your discipline of study, it is what you do with that knowledge that will shape how you get that other piece of paper. Therefore, I start off by talking about ways to help you get your degree.

Before you do anything in the school you choose, you become a student of that school. It is for that reason that being a student should be your most important responsibility. As you settle into your routine and get more involved in different activities, having academics as your core focus will help you be the most successful in getting your degree. This chapter outlines some fundamental things you should do to keep that academic focus amidst all the joys and struggles that college brings. Integrating these behaviors into your daily life will inevitably lead to academic success, keep you in school, and get you your degree.

Be Present in Class

This point may seem obvious, but you would be amazed how easy it is to miss classes in college. If you're in a traditional college setting, the desire to sleep in and miss that 8 a.m. class is a curse that I am sad to say I fell victim to, as many students do. Also present is the temptation to skip your late afternoon class to hang out with friends. Maybe you have an exam in another class, and you think you should skip the class before to prepare for that test. Or you went out the previous night and are too hung over to function in your 10 a.m. class. No matter what the situation, there always seems to be an excuse that justifies not going to class.

Outside the traditional college setting, night school or part-time students face an increasingly difficult struggle making time for classes. These students are typically already working in industry, and the idea of sitting in a classroom after a full 8 or more hours of work is draining just thinking about it. Furthermore, some of these nontraditional students have families they need to tend to, and school means taking time away from them.

In the case of younger children, it can be an effort to attend class while also ensuring their care.

Whether traditional or not, the temptation not to go to class is a very real one. But attending classes is the most important thing you can do in your college career. That is why it is the first part of the first chapter. The advantages gained from going to class are paramount to receiving your degree. Next, I talk about why this is the case and ways to make sure you are present in class without sacrificing the fun and sleep that can keep you from doing just that.

Looking Ahead

Attendance is the easiest, yet most important thing you can do in your job. You may be the most talented employee the company has ever had; but if you don't show up, then nobody can see how you perform, and your absence could result in discipline and potential termination.

Why attend classes? First of all, you're paying for it. Whether it's you or your parents, loans or cash, there is a significant amount of money being spent for you to sit in a hall or at a desk to learn from someone in a class that you signed up for. By not going to class, you're wasting that money—hundreds if not thousands of dollars—and robbing that opportunity from someone who might want to be there more than you do.

Aside from the money you're spending, you miss valuable instruction time. You may be the smartest kid coming out of high school or have years of industry experience, but nobody knows everything. Skipping class because you assume you know so much already is ignorant, and that attitude will prove unsuccessful not only in your academic career, but in your professional life as well. Going to class will give you the chance to learn new things, challenge your own ideas, and make you a more well-rounded person.

While getting the content of your coursework is important, so too is interacting with the person instructing the course. By showing up to class, your professor or instructor sees you and is able to put a face with your name. Face time with these individuals is important, and that face time starts with being present.

Note that I'm suggesting you be present, not just show up. It's easy to show up, but it's another thing to be present. Showing up means that your physical body is in the location it should be at the time it is supposed to be there. Being present is paying attention—not playing on your phone, working on your computer, or sleeping in the back row. By being present and not just showing up, you will digest the information without distractions.

So how do you fight the urge to skip class and make sure that you are present? For starters, think of the pros just discussed and how they outweigh the cons. When you're lying in bed and your conscious is weighing the options, think "I'm better than this. I know what's good for me."

A while ago, I read an article on Reddit® that suggested taking the cost of your tuition for the semester, dividing that cost by the number of classes you're taking, and then considering the dollar amount you're wasting when you skip class. Whenever you're debating whether or not to go to class, think of all the money you would be throwing away by not going. Depending on the school, that money might equal a car payment or a nice night out. Remember: You're in school to be a student, and knowing what you're paying to hold that title will help you ultimately to decide to attend class.

Other habits, such as yielding to peer pressure and sleep, will likely tempt you more than your own internal struggles. The coercion of peers to get you to do stuff besides class can put you on a slippery slope. But keep in mind that they are students just as much as you are. A simple "No, sorry, I've got class" should be enough to get past the temptation; however, if the pressure keeps up, remember the pros and how they out-weigh the cons. Peer pressure indirectly affects sleep as well. You might get convinced to go out or grab a late bite to eat and thereby risk not getting a good night's rest before your morning classes. I'm not saying don't go out and do that, because some of my best memories in college were from late-night conversa-tions with my friends. What I am saying is to be conscious of time and know what you can handle as far as sleep. When you need to get some rest, politely tell your friend or friends that you need to go to bed.

Connect With Your Professors

Because you see them every day when you're present in class, your professors are your most direct source of information about the subjects they teach and the schools they teach at. Some are more willing to help than others, and some may frustrate you to no end when you're trying to get information. In fact, you might feel like you hate some professors by the time you are fin-ished with their classes. But I'm here to tell you that one of the best things you can do is to put these feelings aside and focus on building a connection.

Looking Ahead

In a traditional business setting, you aren't going to pick your boss or your coworkers. Regardless of how you feel about these people, you will have to work with them. By knowing how to appropriately deal with people you don't care for and how to effectively handle conflict, you put yourself at a unique advantage for advancement in your career.

For starters, making connections with your professors can make your academic life much easier. There are vast differences between high school and college, but one key difference is being instructed by a teacher versus a professor. Tweets go viral every year comparing the difference in these roles. Specifically, a student tweets about her strict high school teacher who tells her students that their college professors would never put up with high school antics. This claim is immediately followed by a tweet about a professor dismissing his students early because he doesn't feel like teaching that day. This second tweet often comes as a pleasant surprise to incoming college freshmen because of how true it is.

In general, professors are much laxer than your high school teachers. High school, albeit easy if you want it to be, is very structured in its grading. A set amount of assignments are scored and totaled, and the result is your final grade. College is much different. If your professor has a favorable impression of you, it could be the difference between getting a B or an A. Perhaps even between passing or failing. I received a C instead of a D in a course partly due to the connections I made with my professor. Your academic success can be determined by your interactions with your professors. Making connections with your professors will make you memorable to them when they are grading assignments, issuing final grades, or assigning special projects. Is it necessarily fair? Probably not, but neither is the real world.

Speaking of the real world, making connections with your professors can help you with your career. As I said before, professors are highly knowledgeable about their respective fields. If they were not, they would not be employed by an institution of higher education. Getting any college degree, let alone a master's or doctorate, takes a great deal of time and effort with a subject. Your professors have earned degrees that come with a wealth of knowledge and experience about the industries related to their disciplines. Some of them might have even worked in industry prior to or while completing their graduate studies. As a career-driven college student, making connections with your professors can lead to opportunities in your field. These could include special projects, co-ops, internships, REUs (research experiences for undergraduates), or even a full-time job. If your professor knows you and your intentions for getting a degree, he or she might favor you for these opportunities that could put you on a fast track for your job offer.

So how do you make connections with your professors? For starters, be present in class! While they are teaching, they will likely see your face not sleeping or playing on your phone. This will give them an initially favorable impression of you. Making use of their office hours is another way to build a connection. Some courses can have hundreds of people in them, so that passing glance may not register as much as a personal visit. Most colleges require professors to hold a minimum amount of office hours, so scheduling a meeting during these times (and then going to that meeting) gives you the chance to meet one-on-one with your professors. In that meeting, ask meaningful questions. These questions can be about class, the industry, their life experiences, or just basic small talk. Some questions could be:

- ❖ I'm having some trouble with this assignment. Could you elaborate on what you're looking for?
- ❖ I found this article about this process or innovation in the industry, and I wanted to get your thoughts on it?
- ❖ What made you want to get into this field?
- ❖ Is there anything I could be doing to improve in your class?

The transition from high school to college is one of the biggest changes in a person's life. You are about to be, or are now, a college student and likely an adult by legal definition. In a similar sense, your professor is a human. I believe that humans in general like answering questions they are knowledgeable about, especially about themselves. Think about when a person asks you a question about yourself or asks you for help, and how it heartens you. As an adult, you have the ability to speak to your professors in an adult way, hearten them, and form a meaningful connection. Regardless of how you feel about a professor, making these extra efforts have benefits far too great to pass up. Take advantage of their insight while you can. They might even help you write a book one day!

Build a Peer Network

If you're under the assumption that you can do college alone, I wish you all the best. However, I am here to tell you that college academics are significantly easier with a solid network of peers. Your professors are a great start to your network, but the relationships you have with them are much different than the ones you will have with your peers. Not only will your academic life be much easier while working together with friends in your program, but also you will experience similar struggles as you go through college and into industry following graduation. Your friends will evolve from peers to connections, offering different insights into areas of your field, which you would not otherwise receive.

While I was completing my undergraduate degree, I was very fortunate to have made such good friends within my degree program. We complemented one another's weaknesses and bolstered one another's strengths. The seven of us grew our technical skills, created thorough documentation, warmed up to public speaking, and learned to deconstruct complex problems by approaching them from all angles. For the duration of our time at school, we were a strong team that made the difficult courses like Theory of Computing and Senior Capstone not only seem easy, but almost enjoyable. Finding a team like I did will serve you well when working toward completing your degree.

The first step in building your peer network is to demonstrate your value. When I say "demonstrate value," I am not suggesting you use the targeted, manipulative practices of the D.E.N.N.I.S. System from *It's Always Sunny in Philadelphia*. What I am encouraging you to do is to show your value in class. By being present, you should already be halfway there. Other students who are present in class will recognize your engagement just as you will recognize theirs. While asking questions in class tends to have a negative stigma associated with it, it can help you stand out among your peers by showing that you value your education. Outside of class, be able to complete individual assignments thoroughly and in a timely manner. Being able to effectively work independently will deter you from having to lean on your future teammates. Your peers will look to you for assistance with challenging assignments, and your gracious help will resonate with them. Some classes will form groups on platforms like GroupMe™ or Slack® to disseminate information and message classmates. Either starting these groups or being an active contributor in them demonstrates your ability to be a team player and will make people want to network with you. Lastly and most importantly, be kind to your peers. The Golden Rule tells us to treat others as you would want to be treated. You may very well be the smartest person in your school (and congrats on that, by the way). But nobody wants to work with an a**hole; so be the kind person I know that you are, and people will want to work with you.

Looking Ahead

Most jobs nowadays look for team-driven workers. If you are able and willing to be a team player, you will earn the respect of your teammates, and they will be more likely to reciprocate help should you need it.

Once you've demonstrated your value, it will be easy to pick a strategic network of people to help you with your academic endeavors. Ideally, you want to work with people that do either or both of two things: (a) share your goals, and (b) complement your strengths. If the members of your team have the same goals, achieving them by working together will be easier because you have a common mission. These goals could be to work for a particular organization, live in a certain geographic region, or just to complete the same degree program. Find peers that share your goals and help ensure that the group achieves mutual success.

Equally important to having teammates with similar goals is finding teammates that complement your weaknesses, or "areas of improvement" to use the politically correct terminology. When team members close one another's skill gaps, the result is a completely well-rounded team. While I was capable of doing development work, I knew it was not my best area; whereas I was very good in creating and delivering presentations. I found teammates that were better developers than I was, but weaker presenters. As a result, we produced strong technical projects and presentations to effectively demonstrate our technical work. Take a hard look at yourself and determine your strengths and weaknesses. From there, you can decide what traits to look for in people to form the strongest team.

Note that teams should grow as organically as possible. Walking up to people saying you want to form a strategic team will make you look like Lex Luthor forming the Legion of Doom. Similarly, interviewing people to be on a team will greatly annoy them. Identify people who will help you, but allow those relationships to grow naturally. By doing this, your relationships will become those lifetime college friendships you hear so much about.

Also note that your team should not get to be too big. Inclusivity is important in today's society, and I agree that networking with as many people as possible both within and outside your program is important. Yet, too large of a team can lead to dysfunctional communication, divisive conflicts, and ultimately a deterioration in the work of the entire group. Try keeping your team size to about four to eight people.

You will find opportunities to network with people outside of your program in your extracurricular endeavors. For example, while working on this book, I called on my connections in Education programs to see how they felt about ideas I had, and my friends in English and Liberal Arts programs to help with revisions. These people have been instrumental in helping me succeed, but they were not necessarily in my close team while in school. For those people not in your close team, still make a connection with them. Add them on social media such as LinkedIn® to keep them in your network. Your kindness toward them while in school might lead to mutually beneficial opportunities later on as you each grow in your respective careers.

Humans are inherently social beings, and the successes and struggles faced in college are best shared with a solid network of people. Making connections with your peers will be a great help to you while completing your degree program, whether they are members of your close team or individuals throughout your school. Along the way, these relationships may turn into lifelong friendships. And for those of you who still think you can do it alone, I leave you with a quote from comedian Nick Offerman: "It's a lot better to have eight people with one beer each than to have one dude with eight beers" (assuming you are 21 years old, of course).

Use Your Resources

For the thousands of dollars you spend annually, you tend to get more than just a seat in a lecture hall and a dorm room. Colleges and universities of all sizes offer a great deal of resources to their students, and you can put yourself strategically ahead by taking advantage of them. From your library to wellbeing assistance to career center, identifying these resources and making the effort to use them effectively to your benefit will relieve some of the burden in your academic life, as well as help with your pursuit of two pieces of paper.

Before I go any further, let me clarify the word "use" in this context. When I say "use" in referencing people or things available to you—regardless of whether or not you paid for access to them—I'm not talking about a one-way transaction. It is always important to express gratitude for the services you receive, as well as to offer help whenever you can. Reciprocating assistance is important in life. What you take or use as resources should be with the understanding that you are willing to turn around and help others. This notion is a main reason why I wrote this book: to pay it forward and to use the resources I've been afforded to help others. I hope that as you go through life and find success, you will do the same. At the very least, give a "thank you" to those who are especially helpful to you. Handwritten thank-you notes are still valuable in this technological age.

Libraries

College libraries are very different than high school or public libraries, in size, content, and capacity. Colleges and universities were established to promote higher-level thought in disciplines, and a plethora of knowledge is necessary to foster this intellectual focus. This necessity has resulted in towers of information, both print and digital, made available to students in their respective schools. You, as a student of your school, have access to this tower and all the information therein. Lucky you!

Libraries are important to you as a student for both the information and environment they offer. Your role while in school is centered primarily on being a student and completing your coursework. In addition to your professors and textbooks, the library can offer additional, academically verified information to help you get your work done—such as research for a lab report, sources for a paper, or a reference guide for an unfamiliar programming language. Why would you not take advantage of all the resources available to you in order to do the best possible job, especially if you're paying for the right to use them?

The problem with college libraries is the same problem with Google™: Effectively navigating the resources to find what you're looking for can be difficult, and even intimidating. In the information age, there are seemingly infinite data available to you; and you may know exactly what you need but have no idea how to find or access it. This presumed barrier can cause people to shy away from these resources (it did for me, early on); however, finding what you need is actually very easy with a little help. Librarians are employed by the school to help you find what you need and navigate your school's information systems. Furthermore, Google can be your friend if you curate your search terms to exactly what you're trying to find.

Moreover, within these towers of information are areas to collaborate. As you build your network of peers, you need a place other than your house or dorm to work on group assignments, collaborate on challenging work, or prepare for exams. Most libraries offer private study rooms that you can reserve and use for these purposes. These rooms fill up quickly around midterms and finals, so finding an alternate location to use as a backup is always a good idea. Taking the initiative to coordinate these group efforts, either in the library or another location, will distinguish you as a leader among your peers and prove beneficial when applying for jobs.

Wellbeing Assistance

College can be a stressful time. The college environment, where young people find themselves truly independent for the first time in their lives, provides what I like to call a sandbox for adulthood. Between classes, extracurricular activities, social affairs, on-campus employment, and working toward a career, you can easily lose focus on your own wellbeing. As important as getting your two pieces of paper may be, it is more important to be physically and mentally fit. Colleges and universities recognize this need and have implemented programs to help their students keep a focus on their wellbeing while they get their degrees. If you find yourself facing physical or mental issues, it is in your best interest to look into these programs and make use of them.

One common stereotype of college students is the inevitable "Freshman 15." This extra weight comes as a result of, in part, newfound freedom to eat out whenever you want as well as the "necessity" to eat fast food because of its convenience. Combine those eating habits with increased alcohol consumption (if you're 21 and older), and a sedentary lifestyle and weight gain are practically unavoidable. Aside from weight gain, the communal living situations of college campuses often lead to widespread illness during seasonal transitions. I remember myself and my peers getting sick around the same times every year (usually early October and mid-March), not from a lack of hygiene but from the close proximity to people at almost all times. This means that if someone gets sick, it's likely that everyone will get sick.

To combat these challenges, many campuses have implemented healthy lifestyle programs. These can include various exercise options such as boot camps, Zumba®, and cycling classes. Along with exercising is the importance of healthy eating. On-campus dining options do offer healthy options if you have the willpower to walk past the on-campus Chick-fil-A® and get a nutritious meal from the cafeteria. When those cold and flu seasons come up, health clinics are onsite to help mitigate illness and prevent you from missing class. Being mindful of your physical health by taking advantage of these services and programs will ultimately make you feel better and perform better academically as a result.

In recent years, mental health has become increasingly important in the medical field. The internal pangs brought on by mental illness can feel insurmountable at times and can severely impede academic endeavors. If you are not able to focus or are not feeling engaged in your work, you will not perform as well as you could if those feelings were in your control. Increasingly common diagnoses such as depression and attention deficit disorder can bring on these feelings. Fortunately, most colleges and universities have noticed these problems and have taken steps to help their students with these conditions and accommodate their needs as appropriate. You don't have to be alone in dealing with these problems.

Professional counseling services are available in most colleges and universities either for free or very little cost. Talking to these professionals can help alleviate some of the pressure academic life can bring. Some schools have groups where students with similar ailments can discuss their struggles and how they cope with them. Joining one of these groups not only can help relieve your own pressure, but also can expand your network of peers and assist others in the same situation. Always remember that no problem is so great that it will cause the end of the world. No matter how things may turn out, life will inevitably go on. I charge you to remember to get the help available to you should you need it.

Career Centers

While I realize this chapter is called "Academics," I want to talk briefly about college career centers. Most colleges and universities have some sort of service to help students develop a résumé, prepare for an interview, or get connected with employers. They leverage extensive alumni networks to bring individuals to campus who can help students prepare for the next step in their life and to facilitate meetings with people who have been impressed by graduates of your school and are looking to hire more.

While I hope the contents of this book will be more than sufficient to get you your two pieces of paper, constructive feedback from any source can be helpful. Most career services are free with your tuition, and they are staffed with helpful individuals to review your initial preparations. That double-check could very well be the difference between getting the job you want or not. Furthermore, the representative who works with you might have a connection to help you get to where you want to be. Once you're ready to review your preparations, check your school's website for information on how to schedule an appointment with your career center.

Your college or university likely has other free resources beyond the ones outlined here. Take some time to explore what your school has to offer and take advantage of those resources whenever you can. While working independently is essential to completing your degree, it is also important to know when to ask for help. Higher education is difficult by design; but using the resources your school provides can keep you in the game longer and allow you to get your degree.

Don't Quit

By choosing to read this book, you're probably either in college or have decided you are going there. However, many situations could keep you from getting your degree and even drive you to leave school. *U.S. News and World Report,* widely considered to be a leader in college rankings, published a report saying that one in three college freshmen would not return for their sophomore year[2]. College Atlas reported that 56% of students will drop out of a 4-year program by year 6 of their college career[3]. As I've said before, college is difficult, and people may have to leave for any number of reasons. The previous sections outlined several ways to set yourself up for success in your academic life, but life factors beyond your control can impede your ability to succeed. We will talk about some of these impediments in this section and how to put yourself in a position to keep them from disrupting your plan.

Finances

Unless you have received significant scholarships based on your high school achievements or you have a support system capable of paying for your education, college can be an extreme financial burden. The cost of college in John Mulaney's case was $120,000, and it could be more for you depending on the school. Regardless of how much you are paying or will be paying, you have to know that you are not alone in this struggle. Student loan debt in the United States has reached more than $1.5 trillion dollars[4], and that number will likely increase because more individuals are expected to engage in higher education[5].

If you find yourself in a situation where you need financial assistance in order to earn your degree, you need a plan for how you can work off the accumulated debt. If you can afford one, a financial planner can help you determine how to manage your debt and build a long-term strategy to get out of it. Some campuses have resources to help you understand student loans and to assist with financial planning. If all else fails, the Internet is your friend. The U.S. Government website for student aid assistance is studentaid.ed.gov, which should be your first stop in getting help with finances. Other than that, there are many forums, such as Reddit, that have advice from wise individuals on helping you succeed in eliminating your concerns about debt and focusing on academic success.

Any plan is worthless if you don't stick with it, and the same is true for your plan to control your student debt. Just as public corporations issue quarterly reports on earnings, you too should take a look at your financials every quarter or even every month to gauge where you are at with your plan. If you are using a financial planner or someone at your school, check with that person to find out whether he or she has any suggestions or adjustments. If you're like Jason Derulo and riding solo, apps like ChangEd or Student Loan Hero can help you visualize your situation. Depending on your debt amount and the length of your plan, this review practice might become pretty tedious. When you start to want to give up, think about the relief of being free from financial burden in the end as well as the pride in knowing you stuck with your plan and achieved a long-term goal.

Looking Ahead

Many businesses have both short- and long-term objectives, and both require nearly equal amounts of focus. While most young people can achieve short-term goals, such as completing assignments or preparing for exams, not many experience extensive long-term goals. Being able to say you have completed long-term, plan-driven goals will serve you well when applying for positions and working in industry.

Scholarships are another means to eliminate the burden of student debt. A 2018 study by NerdScholar stated that more than $2.9 billion in federal grant money was unclaimed the prior academic year[6]. Why can't some of that money be yours? If you know you need aid, complete the FAFSA form on the Federal

Student Aid website and see whether you can collect on some of that nearly $3 billion. After completing the FAFSA, look at websites such as BigFuture or BrokeScholar to see whether you qualify for other scholarships or grants. Not only could your search benefit you financially, but also taking the initiative to complete these searches will serve as a talking point when interviewing for jobs.

Building a sound financial plan before your enrollment and keeping up with it throughout your academic career will allow you to finish your degree knowing that you will be able to get sufficient return on your investment. Paying off debt should be easy if you get a good job offer, and I will talk more about that later.

Major Problems

Let's say that you're starting college as an engineering major. You've enjoyed math and science courses through high school, and seeing the median salaries attained by engineering graduates cements your decision to major in that field. As you begin your sophomore year, you begin to take a difficult class that is critical to your future coursework. This class will serve as the foundation for all your future classes and, inevitably, for what you will be doing for your career. Regardless of your efforts in class (being present, talking to your professor, and using your peer network), you continue to struggle and begin to have an existential crisis. Don't worry; you're not alone. Just because you realize you are not in love with what you originally decided to study does not mean you are locked into your decision.

In 2017, the U.S. Department of Education reported that 30% of associate's and bachelor's students changed their major at some point in their college career, and 10% even changed two or more times[7]. While I happened to stick with my major throughout my schooling, there were times when I seriously considered changing and researched those thoughts thoroughly. A number of my friends and even my sister changed their major and were much happier as a result. If you are unhappy in your major, there is never a bad time to switch. One friend I knew was in his senior year of engineering and then switched to professional aviation before graduating. Now, he's in a career where he loves what he is doing. You're not the first person to change your mind, and you certainly won't be the last. Know that whatever you decide, you will be okay in the end.

In my opinion, one of the core reasons people change their major is due to a lack of passion for what they are studying. If you're following what I've outlined in this book so far about keeping an academic focus, then the difficulty in the coursework should not deter you from preparing appropriately. Consider how you feel about going to classes directly in your major and how you feel when you work on assignments within those courses. Are you excited about the problems you are solving or the research you are doing? Or do you feel a sense of agony and resentment? If you don't love, or at least like, what you're doing, it's going to be difficult to stay motivated to complete your work, both now and when you get into industry. While I was engaged in engineering coursework, I was excited to complete the challenging problems in my required courses. Some of my peers did not share my passion, and they struggled in these courses as a result. However, they changed their major to see whether they could find something better and ultimately did. They did not just default to dropping out.

If you are struggling in your major, take a step back from your current situation. Think about why exactly you chose that degree program in the first place. If it was purely for money, then you should probably consider changing. Money is nice and financial stability is important in life. But money is not everything. If you are enjoying what you're doing and passionate about your career, then you will be more motivated to excel and outperform your peers. This will lead to success and consequently more money.

If you've decided to change your major, there are many resources you can use to help you decide where to go next. As part of that self-reflection you're doing, think about what you are passionate about and what you enjoy doing. See whether there is any career that can marry these two areas. I was passionate about cyber security and enjoyed working with computers, so Cyber Engineering was a natural fit. If you need further assistance, the career center at your college should be able to help you decide on a change and will have the resources to help you make the switch. Groups like the College Board® also offer free services to help you decide on a major that is a good fit for you.

After you've made your decision, be confident in it. You should put a lot of thought into changing your major and what you want to change it to. But after it's done, you should keep moving forward and be happy with your choice. Others may frown upon your decision, but it's not theirs to make. It's *your* decision. You decide what you do in life, and you know what makes you happy. And if you decide you aren't happy and want to change again, repeat the process. It's better to take your time and figure out what makes you happy rather than graduate quickly and do something you're going to hate for the rest of your life.

Conflicting Obligations

I've always believed that second to faith in a higher power is the importance of commitment to one's family. If you lose everything else in life, those two things should always be there: God and family. And yet, obligation to family affairs might come as a hindrance to your academic pursuits. Similarly, the commitment to standing employment obligations can take away time that could be dedicated to academic studies. Both of these important obligations may overshadow your academic career and could result in your leaving school.

Let me reiterate that family comes first. You know your family better than I ever could, and you know what situations take precedence over others. Whether a loved one is sick and needs your attention or you need to care for young children, certain responsibilities are clearly more important than your academic career. If this is the case for you, talk with your university about taking a hiatus to handle those responsibilities. However, also make sure that you keep the intent of returning to finish your studies in your mind. It is easy for life to take over and keep us from completing our pursuits. But understanding the benefits that your college degree can offer you and your family should help motivate your return.

Perhaps you do have family obligations, but they do not immediately require your long-term attention. In this case, talk with your family and express how important it is to you to complete your college degree, explaining the benefits the degree will offer the entire family. You have aspirations to build a career from your college experience, so emphasizing how your short-term efforts could lead to longer-term success should help family members support your ambitions. My father completed his master's degree while I was 10 years old. Of course, my two younger siblings and I were upset when he didn't come home at the regular 6:00 p.m. But he made a point to explain to us how great of an opportunity this would be for him as well as how it would help our family. Even at the ages of 10, 8, and 5, we listened to him and understood.

Employment opportunities and obligations can also sideline your academic efforts. It's easy to dedicate more resources to what is giving you money than to something taking it away. After completing my first internship, I enjoyed the steady paycheck so much that I aggressively pursued the opportunity to continue my work while attending school. My manager advised me to focus on school and enjoy that time rather than jumpstarting my career. In hindsight, this might have just been a polite way of saying "no," but his advice was sound for my situation. The value of ultimately completing your degree far outweighs the short-term gains from more immediate employment. Keep that in mind when considering leaving school to begin work. However, if you can balance applicable work experience and your education, then I would advise doing so.

Perhaps you are an unconventional student, meaning you started work, but are now going to school to further your career opportunities. Some employers offer tuition reimbursement for those working to complete a degree. If your employer does that, make sure you understand the policies regarding this benefit. Otherwise, you might find yourself ultimately footing the bill and in need of reviewing the book's section on how to pay for college. It is also important that your manager or supervisor understands your academic pursuits. If that person is aware of your efforts, he or she can work with you to make sure your job commitments are fulfilled while you work to complete your degree. Your employer ultimately benefits from your getting a degree as much as you do, because the result is a more skilled worker. Leverage this point in your discussion.

Looking Ahead

Many career roles in the modern era involve juggling multiple tasks and projects. Having that ability will help you stand out among your colleagues and will lead to more responsibility, which will help advance your career.

The major takeaway when dealing with current obligations is the need for communication. You need to communicate the value a college degree adds for you. It's up to you to communicate with the appropriate parties about your endeavors, and then to manage your standing responsibilities while completing your degree. Family and work are important, but ultimately finishing your degree and not quitting will bode well for both.

Leaving college is difficult for both you and society. Momentum in your academic pursuits is difficult to rekindle once it is lost. Stan Jones, the former president of Complete College America™, stated, "Many students who return to college end up quitting again." Furthermore, students who quit school end up costing taxpayers an estimated $3 billion per year in accrued debt from federal and state education subsidies.[8] Do your best to stick with your plan and stay focused on completing your degree while you're enrolled. On their death beds, people often regret what they did not do more than they regret what they did. Don't let your college degree be one of those things you regret not doing.

Never Stop Learning

Growing up, my Grandma Peg always told me, "You should learn something new every day." She's told me a lot of crazy things, but this was not one of them. You learn a lot while in college, both in the classroom and in life. It's arguably one of the biggest periods of growth in a person's life. However, the learning should not stop once you walk across the stage. In fact, some of these additional learning opportunities can occur while you're still in school. I will talk later about opportunities to supplement your education that can place you in a strategic advantage when looking for employment, as well as about continuing to learn after completing your degree.

Certifications

If there is one thing that I stressed more than anything to my friends in school, it was the importance of certifications. Not only does the learning associated with certifications offer great information about current industry practices, but it also can be the difference between you or somebody else getting the job of your dreams. During my first internship, I studied for and received the CompTIA Network+ and Security+ certifications—two entry-level IT certifications that cost me around $600 at the time. These two certifications helped distinguish me from my peers and propelled me to two more internships with two different companies as well as to my full-time role upon graduation. In my opinion, there is no quicker return on investment than that of certifications.

Most degree programs do not directly incorporate certifications into their coursework. For that reason, you should take the initiative to look into what certifications are relevant in your industry. Search "certifications for [insert your major here]" and see what results come up. Depending on what you are studying, there might be a great number of certifications to pursue. Your professors should be able to help you discern which ones are appropriate for you. If you're studying engineering, you'll likely need to pass the Fundamentals of Engineering (FE) exam. Accountants and financial advisors need to pass the CPA and CFA, respectively. If you're still unsure about what certifications would be best as an entry-level candidate, check with your career center or query online forums like Reddit to get some more information.

Once you've decided what certifications are right for you, determine which study materials you should use. Certifications are meant to expand your knowledge of an industry and to demonstrate that you have knowledge of information based on certain objectives. By looking at these certification objectives, you might be able to identify courses at your school that could help you learn the material needed to pass the certification exam. Community or junior colleges sometimes offer courses or boot camps dedicated to the content of certifications. Additionally, Amazon™ has an extensive library of study guides and practice questions for an assortment of certifications. Content creators on YouTube™ also offer free resources that teach you the material you need to pass the certification exam. Whichever way you elect to prepare, studying before your certification exam is critical. Otherwise you might find yourself shelling out thousands of dollars until you pass the test.

Speaking of costs, certification exams can get expensive. Remember that certifications at this point in your life are an investment more than a requirement. The $600 I spent in 2015 translated into thousands of dollars in wages from later positions. Look up the cost of certifications and come up with a plan for how to pay for them. When interviewing for internships or co-op positions, ask your interviewer whether there is an opportunity to earn a certification as part of the position. The question will show an interviewer that you care about your preparation for the position as well as your future in the industry; and, if they say yes, then you'll have the payment for your certification secured. Even if your employer can't pay for your certification, it is still worthwhile for you to invest your own resources to obtain it. Dipping into your savings or working a part-time job to pay for certifications will be a temporary setback for a solid return when the job hunt begins.

Certifications set you apart not only based on the qualifications they represent, but also because they show that you care about your industry enough to gain higher knowledge of it. The information you learn from certifications can also help with your coursework. After taking the Network+ and Security+ exams, I found a great deal of my course material was related to what I learned studying for those two tests. Do yourself a favor and look into certifications; I guarantee any costs will be outweighed by the benefits.

Reading

If you told 12-year-old Skyler that he would be writing a book promoting reading for fun, he would probably call you an idiot (he's not a very nice kid). I used to loathe reading and, to some degree, I still do. But a while ago I had a realization that most of my generation focuses on getting information from videos of less than 5 minutes in length that can be digested without direct attention. Having the patience to read a book teaches discipline, not to mention the contents of the book itself. Furthermore, I realized that the reason I hated reading was because I was being told to read books on subjects I did not care about. I'll take a movie over a novel any day of the week; but nothing in my opinion compares to some quality nonfiction, especially books that help you grow as a person.

Although finding time to read while completing your coursework is difficult, books outside the scope of your major, your industry, or your belief system can significantly expand your intellect. Being knowledgeable on a breadth of topics can help inform your opinions and allow you to solve complex problems. Your informed opinions and solutions will likely translate into your being viewed as a thought leader, as well as help you formulate intelligent responses to interview questions. Expanding your intellect through reading also frees you from ignorance and can make you more empathetic. Whether the content is physical or digital, make an effort to do some outside reading for about half an hour a day. I like to do this before bed, because it's a very relaxing way to unwind at the end of the day.

I have listed a series of my personal recommendations in the back of this book. For other recommendations, get advice from people you view as mentors. They either will have written a book or will recommend books they are reading or have read. Of course, there are also lists like those from *The New*

York Times and Amazon, where you can find the top books on the market. You'll be surprised how much you will distinguish yourself from your peers by reading a book instead of watching a video. If anything, do it to prove 12-year-old Skyler wrong.

Graduate Degrees

Let's fast forward a couple years and assume that you've received your two pieces of paper. While you've had great success in your undergraduate career, going on to receive a graduate degree can further extend your success. A study conducted by Georgetown University in 2015 found that individuals with a graduate degree earned, on average, $17,000 more annually than those without one[9]. Furthermore, a graduate degree allows you to specialize in your role in industry beyond your undergraduate degree. For example, if you receive an undergraduate Computer Science degree, you can specialize in application development with a master's degree in Software Engineering or an MBA in technology management. Ultimately, it's up to you to decide how you want to shape your career. It's a step outside of the sandbox, and deciding to go to play kickball or go on the jungle gym. You're still playing, but now you get more of a choice in what you want to play.

Assuming you are successful in getting your two pieces of paper and are working for a good company, your employer might offer tuition reimbursement for your graduate degree in exchange for a certain time commitment, usually around 2 to 3 years. This should not be a problem, because staying with a company for at least a couple years is important to reflect your ability to remain committed to a group. If you are working full-time, graduate programs also tend to be very flexible. My father completed his master's degree in night classes. He would complete his work during the day and then go to school at night. Earning another degree is a sacrifice, but it can further expand your opportunities for career growth.

Living in the information age is both a blessing and a curse. We are privileged to have access to any information we want or need almost instantaneously. Yet, if you become complacent in what you know, then you will likely fall behind. There is an old saying that you have to crawl before you can walk, and I am a proponent of that kind of continual development and growth. However, you can crawl faster than your peers, and you can learn to walk faster than your superiors. Continuously learning will help you crawl faster and walk quicker, meaning that it will help you advance more quickly in your career. It will also make Grandma Peg very happy that you're learning something new every day.

Ask the Experts

Dr. Jenna Carpenter, Dean of Engineering at Campbell University

I had the privilege of having Dr. Carpenter as an instructor for a freshman seminar and a Calculus class. In both of these classes, Dr. Carpenter exemplified what it truly means to thrive in the academic arena. She has become a champion for STEM (science, technology, engineering, and mathematics) education, particularly for women, and has hosted a TEDx Talk on that subject. I hope that Dr. Carpenter's words will motivate you in your academic endeavors just as she motivated me as I began my college career. **Tell us a little about yourself, your career path, and what you currently do.**

Before becoming Dean of Engineering, I had a rather circuitous career path, which is not particularly uncommon as a woman in a STEM (science, technology, engineering, and mathematics) field. All of my degrees are in Mathematics. While the doors of engineering were technically "unlocked" when I started my undergraduate career, they weren't necessarily "open," welcoming, or supportive. The philosophy in engineering education back then was still very much a weeding-out process. Faculty literally tried to run off as many students as possible in as many different ways as possible. Being a woman was just another reason to kick you out the door. Consequently, like a number of other women my age, I came to engineering through the back—and far more welcoming—door of mathematics.

I spent a decade as an Engineering Department head and 8 years as an associate dean before "retiring" from my previous institution and moving to Campbell University to become its founding Dean of Engineering. Building an engineering school from scratch, in a region bursting with opportunities in engineering, was simply an opportunity I could not pass up. Here, I have the flexibility to create a program that trains students for 21st-century careers using methods such as hands-on, project-based learning, which incorporate professional development and service learning. The role allows me to use the wide variety of skills and experiences I have accumulated to educate a diverse cohort of students. It is a complex and enormous task, but no 2 days are the same, and I am certainly not bored!

An article published by *The Huffington Post* in 2014 and updated in 2017 was titled in part "7 Reasons Why You Shouldn't Go to College ."[10] There seems to be an increas-

ing camp of those advising against a college education. What would you say in rebuttal to these nay-sayers?

Those that advise against college are shortsighted and confuse a college degree with job training. Don't get me wrong; a college degree should equip you to be employed, but it provides far more than job training, which can be particularly ephemeral. College prepares you for a *career,* not a *job.* There is a huge difference. When you are prepared for a career, you are far more flexible and able to weather the whims of the economy. If all you receive is job training, then you are out of luck when those skills become obsolete or the industry changes. Change will occur at a much faster pace over the next 50 years than it has over the last 50. A career provides you with a life path or two. You are capable of growth and change, better prepared for advancement and leadership, among other benefits.

Even beyond the career preparation that a college degree provides, college also provides you with an education. Being educated means you are capable of thinking for yourself, as opposed to relying on leaders who spoonfeed you their personal, and often self-serving, agendas. It means that you have the skills—and hopefully the drive—to continue to learn, grow, and mature throughout your life. You have perspective, understanding, and appreciation for culture, the arts, history, and many other subjects that mere job training ignores. You are a more sophisticated communicator, better at analysis and problem-solving, have stronger interpersonal skills—all of which come in handy in life in general, not just at work.

The list goes on and on. In short, you are prepared to live a far better life—one that equips you to be employed, certainly, but also one that equips you to use your skills, talents, interests, and opportunities to make the world in general, as well as your little corner of it, a better place.

What was the hardest course you took in your undergraduate career? Did you fail it? How did you handle that rigor?

I have a lifetime 4.0 average, so I haven't ever failed a course. I did take a senior-level biomedical engineering controls course the last quarter of my undergraduate career that was a real challenge. The official prerequisites for the course listed only differential equations, which I had taken as a math major; however, in reality, there were a number of upper-level engineering courses that were needed that everyone else in the class—all seniors and graduate students in biomedical or chemical engineering—had taken. I was lost; and the course was very poorly taught, so everyone else was lost as well. I worked extremely hard and pulled out an A in the end, but it made the last quarter of my undergraduate career a nightmare.

As an educator, what are some of the habits you see trending from some of your more successful students?

I have been teaching freshmen STEM majors for more than 30 years. Half of what I am trying to teach has nothing to do with the course content. If they want to succeed, students have to grow up once they get to college. Many bright kids fail because they won't listen, follow directions, discipline themselves to study and keep up with their assignments, be proactive in getting their questions answered, and so forth. It's really just the basics, but many smart students have never had to really work hard in high school, and they want to keep making As with minimal effort. To succeed really just takes hard work along with taking ownership of your own education. If I can get my students to cross that bridge during their first semester, then I know that their odds of graduating are very high.

In contrast, what are some habits you see from lower performers, and how would you suggest mitigating them?

This goes back to my previous answer. Weaker students tend to be immature, have a poor work ethic, and are often stubborn. They try to do things their way instead of following advice or doing what they are asked to do the way they are asked to do it; they also try to figure it out on their own instead of seeking help. Students have to work out how to manage their time, motivate and discipline themselves, and listen. Asking for help isn't a sign of weakness. In today's world, you aren't going to succeed as a lone wolf. You have to learn to work as part of a team, ask questions, solve problems, and so forth.

You have a passion for women in STEM, and your TEDx Talk outlines some of the early biases that instill doubt in girls who are excited about STEM fields[11]. Speaking to both young men and women who are about to enter the working world, what would you suggest to them as a means of overcoming these biases and helping to create a more inclusive workplace?

No one likes to be boxed in or limited by stereotypes, and stereotypes from our culture are what fuel implicit biases. If you want to create a more inclusive workplace on all fronts, learn all you can about (your) implicit biases, along with simple strategies for managing around them. Research clearly and repeatedly has shown that we all have implicit biases—so ignoring them or denying their existence is pointless and immature—and they extend to pretty much everything in our lives, not just women in

STEM. We all need to realize that our implicit biases color our perspectives and cloud our judgment. The more we are aware of them, the more likely we are to catch ourselves and self-correct so that they don't lead us astray.

I remember in several of your lectures you quoted Isaac Newton and how he and his work "stood on the shoulders of giants." Who are your giants, and what did you learn from them to help with your success?

I have benefited from a number of mentors over my career, from faculty during my undergraduate and graduate days to peers over the span of my career who advocated for and encouraged me. At times, they saw potential in me that I had not yet recognized in myself. At other times, they spurred me to pursue opportunities or reach for loftier goals. We all need people around us to encourage us, give us a nudge from time to time, and believe in us. Those are the most valuable things that my giants have done for me.

What lasting advice would you give young people starting their college and professional careers?

My mother wasn't really one for giving advice, but once she told me that she could have never envisioned the opportunities that she would have in her lifetime. She grew up on a small family farm in northern Arkansas during the Great Depression, graduating high school on the eve of World War II. The world was about to change in unprecedented ways, so she was right. She couldn't have possibly foreseen how the world would change in her lifetime—and she lived to just a few days short of her 93rd birthday. Her advice to me, and mine to young people, is to take advantage of every opportunity that you can. Not just in your classes, but on the campus or in your community as a whole. Go to plays and concerts, take courses, learn new skills or hobbies, hear distinguished lecturers, visit historic sites, turn down no opportunity to travel, join and be active in student organizations, and volunteer (virtually no group ever has enough volunteers).

These experiences will provide part of that education that I talked about before. They will help you develop broader—and nontechnical—skill sets. You never know when these lagniappe (Louisiana-speak for "a little something extra") experiences will be what distinguishes you from the pack, what gives you an edge, or what helps you make connections and understand "the whole" better than your peers. These experiences will also make sure you have a life well-lived. Take advantage of every opportunity, create opportunities—that's my parting advice.

Wrap-Up

Rapper Denzel Curry sings in his song "Ultimate" that you'd "better learn something and get a degree." Although he did not go to college, he's not wrong. Having an academic focus while you complete your degree should be preeminent. This requires you not only to show up to class, but also to be present in your studies. Beyond that, networking with both your professors and peers provides a strategic advantage to help you manage your coursework and lay the groundwork for your career. Take advantage of the abundance of free resources your school has to offer. No matter how tough it may seem, don't quit, because it will be even harder to start back up. In fact, don't stop learning or you will fall behind. Following this advice will hopefully help you get one of your two pieces of paper, making you a college graduate and setting you up to be an "Ultimate" employee.

Chapter 2

Extracurriculars: Making the Most of Your One-Way Ride

Your degree alone will not get you a job out of college. You could graduate with a perfect 4.0 GPA and be objectively the smartest person to ever graduate from your school, but there will likely be people with GPAs lower than yours who will get a job instead of you. Academics are important, but employers do not evaluate your candidacy based purely on your academic achievement. Laszlo Bock, Google's SVP (senior vice-president) of people operations, said in an interview that "GPAs are worthless as criteria for hiring." I believe this to be true if only for one reason: The way you perform in an academic setting is different than how you perform in a professional work setting.

Academics are generally evaluated on a 100-point scale from A to F. You are graded from that scale based on how you complete certain criteria of an assignment, project, or exam. The real world does not work that way. Industry work, by comparison, operates on a pass-fail basis. Either you complete your job successfully or you fail to achieve the desired results. What this means is that unlike just taking a B in a class and moving on, you have to strive for an A every day you show up for work or risk underperforming, which could sacrifice advancement opportunities or bonuses, or even get you fired.

One of the biggest hurdles I hear from my peers when I help them with a résumé or job application is that they don't have the real-world experiences they need to get the job they want. It's a chicken-and-egg scenario where you need 1–2 years of experience to get a job, but you can't get the experience without first getting the job. While you might not be able to get legitimate work experience, the truth is that you are able to get those skills employers are looking for while you're in school. You don't need any prior experience to get those skills. The trick is to leverage extracurricular activities.

Extracurricular activities, or ECs as I will call them, provide you the opportunity to take a break from the rigors of academic life. Your time spent in ECs allows you to participate in activities with individuals who have beliefs, interests, and motivations similar to your own. Lack of involvement outside of your regular classes can make you bored and complacent, and might even lead to your dropping out. Various organizations operate more like real-world businesses than your classes and can give you those marketable skills and pass-fail opportunities that employers can then use to evaluate how you will perform in their company. This chapter discusses the different types of ECs you can partake in while in college, both professional and recreational. Specifically, you will explore what the activity is, why you should join, and how you can leverage your EC participation into marketable skills for employers.

Student Employment

I understand this might seem a little out of place because it is "employment," but EC in this case means any activity not specific to your academic career. Student employment does not necessarily count as career development because your role is not necessarily reflective of your pursued degree. Instead, you could serve as a receptionist for your college or an administrator, a tutor for your younger peers, an IT rep helping with your school's network, or perhaps another position. Maybe your student employment comes from outside your college or university, meaning you work as a server or do data entry at a company. Regardless of what it is, you should make an effort to have some sort of employment during your academic pursuits.

The advantage to this work, aside from the presumed pay, is that it will give you a taste of what the working world will be like. As stated before, working in industry and working in academics are very different arenas, and getting the experience of working in a student employment position will help you transition into an internship or full-time opportunity. Furthermore, the skills you gain in these positions are also some of the easiest to craft into strong points for your résumé.

Seeking out and applying for these positions is almost as advantageous as the experience you'll gain from actually performing the job. Taking the initiative to follow leads from your peers or going to different offices on or around your campus is a skill you will need in your later job searches. Depending on your school, there could be hundreds, if not thousands, of students looking for employment. Putting in the extra effort to get that job will set you apart from those other students. While I got my student employment through a company I interned for, I still had to seek out the opportunity. After visiting the lab for the first time, I emailed the professor and company liaison in charge of the lab and asked whether I could work in the space. They both agreed, and I ended up working in that lab for the remainder of my college career.

Looking Ahead

Initiative is one of those skills that's almost impossible to teach, but it's coveted by any team if you can learn it. Being able to rely on someone to take action on his or her own and then get the job done is not only appreciated, but can quickly lead to career advancement.

Once you're in your role, go above and beyond what you're required to do. Go the extra mile where you can, take on additional tasks if possible, and do the things that you or your teammates do not necessarily want to do. Ask questions of your boss and coworkers and see where you can improve as well as what strengths you can build on. This approach will not only give you more work experience, but also expand your network. In addition, it will show your supervisor that you're a dedicated worker and make it easier to request a letter of recommendation when the time comes to apply for internships or jobs. I made a point to go above and beyond in my role by taking tasks that were mundane (documenting processes), perplexing (coming up with technical solutions to be applied to course curriculum), and awkward (having difficult conversations with my superiors in order to solve work-related problems). Doing the same in your student employment will serve you well.

Looking Ahead

At some point in your career, you are likely to encounter office drama. If it does not involve you, your best bet is to just ignore it and move on with your work. If it does involve you, work to understand the other side and address the issue directly. This action will show your maturity and ability to resolve conflicts.

If you can get some work experience while in school, take that opportunity. No matter how menial it might be, the experience will be worthwhile and help to give your résumé the meat it needs to be worthwhile to recruiters. The experience, when presented in the right way, will work as the entrée to the side dishes of your other ECs.

Professional Societies

While your student employment experience might not be directly related to your major, participation in a professional society can connect you with other people in your field of study.

These organizations are generally made up of both college students and working professionals, and requirement for membership usually involves attending a weekly or monthly meeting along with a small fee. If you're going to college for a career, joining a professional society for your field of study is critical both for academic and career purposes.

From an academic perspective, professional societies give you a chance to network with students and professionals in your field. These people are likely taking the same courses as you, or have taken them already, and could potentially be a part of your circle while you all work on your undergraduate degree. These organizations also give you the chance to meet upper-level students in your field of study. Although not by much, they still have more experience than you. Taking advice from these individuals will not only help you in your academic endeavors, but also give you insight on future opportunities in your field when they graduate.

Larger professional societies have national conferences annually that give you a chance to learn more about the industry, meet people in your program from other schools, and network with working professionals in your field. As mentioned in the previous chapter, it is critical to always be learning, and conferences like these give you the chance to learn about the current state of your industry through panels, keynotes, breakout sessions, and networking events. Being engaged in conference events and learning as much as you can about the state of your field can enlighten you about skill gaps your industry needs to fill; targeting these areas can set you apart from your peers when applying for future employment.

Looking Ahead
Depending on your field, your employer might send you to an annual conference to learn more about the industry, develop skills, and find new ways to improve the business. While it's important to have fun during these times away from the office, you should take in as much knowledge as you can—not only to help yourself, but also your company.

Some schools' degree programs are ranked higher than others. Because of this, learning from your peers in other schools can be very helpful; you can consider different approaches to your studies when completing your coursework. These conferences often come in the midst of the academic year. Bringing problems or assignments that your intercollegiate peers can help with presents a unique opportunity to get outside advice on your work, as well as network with colleagues from other schools. Similarly, offer your peers assistance wherever you can. You'll establish a new connection and build some political capital with the assistance you disseminate.

Probably the most important benefit of these conferences is the opportunity to meet professionals working in your industry. Conversations with these individuals, either through asking questions at events or speaking with them one-on-one, create a connection with individuals who are where you want to be upon graduation. These people can help you get to where you want to be, and they will be eager to help you if you approach them the right way. The mentorship, insights, and opportunities a person in industry can give you while in college are invaluable. While I was fortunate enough to have found this mentorship in my father, industry conferences offer you a venue to interact with these potential mentors in a more relaxed setting than a career fair or interview.

To find a professional society in your field, ask your professor to recommend an organization appropriate for you. While there might not be a professional society specifically related to your major, your professor or mentor can point you to one that gives you access to the advantages previously mentioned. These organizations generally hold open meetings at least once a term, usually at the beginning of the term, if not more frequently. Attend the open meeting, pay the small fee, then attend the member meetings regularly. Find ways to get involved either by serving as an officer or taking the lead on special projects. Your leadership and actions in these roles are what you can convert to that coveted real-world experience.

Looking Ahead

Taking on special projects gives you another avenue for continuous learning. A lead role on a successful special project within your business could translate to career advancement, promotion, and likely even more new experiences.

If your school does not have a professional organization for or related to your major, you may consider starting one. I graduated with a degree in Cyber Engineering, a program that was first of its kind in the country. As such, there was no national professional society for my peers and me, but there was one started locally: the Association of Cyber Engineers. It provided an opportunity for students in cyber engineering to network with one another, learn relevant skills, and listen to guest speakers working in industry. While I was not a leader in that organization, I was good friends with those who were. All were endowed with technical, presentation, and interpersonal skills that set them apart from other cyber engineering students, resulting in their employment at elite government agencies and international corporations. If you are interested in starting a professional organization or a local chapter of an existing one, work with your school's Office of Student Affairs and find out what you need to do to set up the organization. Again, these skills can be translated into marketable experience.

Professional societies afford you both academic and career advantages. Use these groups as an opportunity to network with your peers, both in your college and around the world. Attend conferences and absorb as much information and meet as many people as you can. Take on leadership opportunities in the organization or start one if your school doesn't have one for your field. Most importantly, make note of everything you do in and for the organization, because these experiences will help you fill your supposed skill gaps.

Service Organizations

While professional societies give you a means of building skills related to your field, service organizations give you a means of identifying things you care about outside of work. They are groups where you volunteer your time to support your passions while meeting and working with others who feel the same as you. They give recruiters and interviewers a look inside your personality and what you value in life, as well as provide you a means of giving back. Groups like these include:

- ❖ Religious (Baptist Collegiate Ministry, Muslim Students' Association)
- ❖ Political (College Democrats or Republicans, Young Americans for Liberty)
- ❖ Charitable (Habitat for Humanity, St. Jude Up 'til Dawn, Humane Society)
- ❖ Academic (tutoring at a local elementary school)

I imagine that to get into the school you are attending (or will attend), your application was based on being a well-rounded person (unless your mom was Aunt Becky in *Full House*). The same is true when applying for jobs. Every company I have worked for has placed a major emphasis on service and outreach, including as much as a paid day off to give back to the community. An orientation for one of my internships ended with 2 hours of a community service project sorting crayons that would be melted down into new crayons for kids in need. It was a chance not only to do some good for the community, but also to have fun with the people who would be my peers for the next 3 months.

The decision to join one of these organizations starts with a moment of self-reflection. These organizations should not simply be a box to check, but an extension of your passions and beliefs. You have to genuinely believe in what your chosen service organization stands for, or potential employers will see through your hypocrisy and consequently be turned off to hiring you. My advice would be to take some time and think about what makes you mad, particularly in the news. For me, it's stories about animal abuse and childhood illness, but for you it might be opioid addiction, homelessness, education, or another topic that grinds your gears.

Once you find your passions, find the groups that align with those passions. These could include examples mentioned here, but check with your Office of Student Affairs for a list of all registered organizations on your campus along with contact information of a representative who can help you join. Like the professional societies, you can of course go through the steps to start your own service organization on your campus. A good friend of mine helped start a chapter of Young Americans for Liberty, a libertarian political group, on our campus. He told me that the experience was very worthwhile in his efforts to enter politics, from attending national conferences to networking opportunities he would have otherwise not been able to experience.

Like the advice given for professional societies, you should get involved in projects for your service organization as well. Heavy involvement or a leadership role in a project within these organizations carries experience you can sell on a résumé. That being said, also use your involvement in service organizations to appreciate the unique opportunity you have to go to college. In October 2017, it was estimated that one in three high school graduates between the ages of 16 and 24 was not enrolled in college[12]. Service organizations give you a chance to give back as a result of the opportunities you have, and ideally your involvement will build a strong foundation for your service throughout your career.

Greek Life

In my opinion, becoming a Greek-affiliated student is one of the most important things you can do to develop your career.

This might come across as a bold statement, especially considering negative headlines regarding binge drinking and hazing. Some of my strongest leadership skills came out of being a part of my Greek organization, and they're attainable by you as well. In fact, even the negatives of Greek life that I mentioned have a place in your career development.

National fraternities and sororities, like corporations and businesses, are mission-driven. Their mission is to develop collegiate men and women into better people through camaraderie and belief in certain core values, which are specific to each Greek organization. Furthermore, each chapter (your school's group of that national fraternity or sorority) works as a branch office for that organization. Your chapter's membership works to advance and execute the mission of your organization, meaning that you all work together to develop one another. How do you do that? Through not only social activities, but also leadership development seminars, academic assistance, service outreach events, philanthropy, and the network of brothers and sisters to fall back on when life gets challenging. We've talked about college being difficult, and the advantages of Greek life really come through at the most challenging of times.

Being a Greek student also opens the doors to an extensive group of alumni, both within your respective organization and among Greek alumni as a whole. Some organizations have been around for more than a century, meaning there are potentially hundreds of thousands of people who share the same core beliefs as you working in industry right now. During my internship in North Carolina, 800 miles away from my chapter at Louisiana Tech, I happened to wear a polo with my fraternity insignia on it. On that day, two different people approached me who were alumni from my fraternity. We had a great conversation about our times as part of our respective chapters, and each of us walked away knowing that we had made a worthwhile connection.

Even if you and another individual are not in the same Greek organization, there is still a mutual respect within the greater Greek community for one another's values and work ethic. I remember speaking with a company VP about the future of one of the projects I had worked on for several years while at school; we ended up discussing the value of hiring Greek students purely because of the advantages Greek students offer.

The advantages I'm referring to are the soft skills acquired through general Greek activities, and these relate to the corporation analogy I made earlier. The weekly meetings of your Greek chapter are comparable to staff meetings, town halls, or stand-ups. The practice of talking to people you don't know during recruitment and making good conversation with them quickly is transferrable to professional networking and interacting with coworkers with whom you might not regularly work. You are also expected to have respect for your organization by doing small things like not drinking while wearing your organization's insignia, just as you should represent your company well in public. All of these things build a sense of professionalism that will carry over into your working life.

Looking Ahead

Drinking at workplace functions is a very touchy topic. You absolutely should not drink at office events if you're under the age of 21. If you are of age, it's important to self-moderate so that you don't end up acting like a fool and possibly damaging your career potential. Eat before and while drinking, space drinks with a glass of water, and limit your alcohol intake to 2–3 drinks. No night of drinking is worth sacrificing your career.

As I said before, advantages can also be derived from the presumed negatives of Greek life, specifically hazing. Let me be clear: I am against hazing that places individuals in a clear and present physical, mental, or emotional danger—including abuse of alcohol, beatings, obstacle courses, or any combination of these, among other hazardous activities. The positive "hazing" that I'm referring to falls outside the scope of the regular definition of that term. Positive hazing includes things like dress codes, being required to dress professionally and understanding that dress codes might be a part of your role. Having to bring items like manuals and materials to meetings or training are habits transferrable between pledging and the corporate world. While these things might be considered hazing, Greek life gives you a means of trying and failing in an environment where doing so is inconsequential to your career goals.

The opposite of being a pledge is to serve on the executive council, where aside from the generic leadership experience you get from general Greek life, you learn a very unique skill that is invaluable in the real world: how to fail. While failure is common for all college students, as mentioned in the sandbox analogy, executive council members are more susceptible to failure. When you are on the executive council of your respective Greek organization, you are not only in charge of some of your best friends, but you are also in charge of a group of 18–23-year-old college students. With that comes handling the frankly stupid actions of some members, managing difficult conflicts, and still maintaining the friendships you cherish while being a fair leader. With all of this, you are almost assured to fail at something, but that is okay.

In the 2009 movie *Star Trek*, there is a scene where Kirk handles a seemingly impossible challenge with ease while in flight school. After the challenge, it is revealed by Spock that the task is designed to be impossible in order to teach cadets how to thrive under pressure and handle imminent failure. I use Spock's challenge as a metaphor for serving on the executive council. Absent of something criminal, your failing as an executive council member will not be the end of the world; in fact, failing to act effectively in your position, at times, will make you a stronger leader. Much like college is a sandbox for adulthood, the executive council is a sandbox for corporate leadership.

Looking Ahead

Knowing how to handle failure is almost equally as important as succeeding. Nobody is perfect, and the corporate world knows that. A saying I've heard recently in the working world is "failing fast and failing safe." Your knowing how to do that is important and will bode well for your success.

Aside from the professional benefits, I would be remiss if I did not mention the friendships you make in Greek life. Speaking for myself, some of my best friends are people I met during my 4 years as part of my Greek organization. Through the good times and the bad times, these are the people I have turned to and who have turned to me for advice, support, or just to be there when we needed someone. I trust them with my life, and I'm sure you will find the same in your Greek experience.

Involvement in Greek life depends initially on your school. Some schools allow all students to participate in fall recruitment; however, others may require first-year students to wait until spring semester, giving students time to get their bearings in college life before entering Greek life. Whenever you're allowed to go through rush (the recruitment process), contact your Interfraternity Council (IFC) for guys and Panhellenic Council for girls to get more information. Recruitment can be very stressful, but it's an experience you'll look back on as worthwhile (it might even be your first experience in speed networking). Note that most schools still use a mutual-selection process for recruitment, meaning both you and the organization select each other. This means that if for whatever reason the organization of your choice does not select you, then you'll default to your second or third choice. So, it is important that you sell your best self through the recruitment process, much like you will in interviewing with companies.

In the event that you do not get selected to join a Greek organization, do not be discouraged. Rejection is tough, but it's not the end of the world. Contrary to popular belief, Greek life continues to expand on college campuses across the country. Contact an organization that is not already on your campus and see whether they can help you start a colony (new chapter) at your school. You'll get the benefits of serving on the executive council combined with those of founding an organization. This is a great deal of work, and you must be prepared for the challenges associated with starting a chapter. My sister was a founding member of her organization, and nearly 3 years later they still have their challenges. If you're willing to put in the effort, starting a colony can greatly benefit you as you prepare to apply for jobs.

I hope this section has helped not only convey the positive aspects of Greek life, but also address some of the negatives that dominate the news. Greek life can be a positive experience if you join the organization that fits you and can add a tremendous amount of value to your college career, employment opportunities, and personal life.

Building Your Package

These ECs are only a sliver of those you can participate in during your college career, but they were chosen based on both my personal experience with them as well as the value they added in developing my professional experience. But the question still stands: How do these extracurricular activities add value? How does planning a debate for College Democrats or helping with a fraternity fundraiser add value to your potential employment? This section discusses leveraging those seemingly irrelevant experiences in organizations into marketable skills that will set you apart when applying for internships and jobs later on.

The first thing I would suggest is to research the jobs you want. Look at what skills individuals currently working in these roles have and determine which ECs will help you obtain those skills. The earlier you do this, the more time you will have to get an adequate amount of experience in those areas. With the right experience, you can become more attractive to recruiters for the jobs you want. I discuss more about job hunting later, but for now just look into roles at a high level.

Looking Ahead

A 2018 study by Deloitte found that 43% of millennials will likely leave their role within 2 years, and 61% of Gen Z workers would do the same.[13] While leaving a role for a better opportunity can be exciting, it's important to ensure that you have the skills to perform well in that new role. Pivoting, the ability to adapt, requires researching the functions of that new role and then obtaining the needed skills to help boost your career.

Though ECs can be valuable, it is important that you not overextend yourself. One key thing I learned during my freshman year was during a lecture segment on T-shaped people. Being a T-shaped person means having a breadth of experiences at a shallow level, represented by the top line of the T, but having depth of experience in one area, represented by the vertical portion of the T[14]. Being T-shaped allows you to pick your top 1–2 passions and build the bulk of your experiences there, while still participating in areas of lesser interest.

Your T is entirely up to you, and it helps define you as an individual. Maybe your T emphasizes experience in a professional society, while another person may find more value in a service organization. Personally, I spent a great deal of my time focusing on Greek life and my student employment, and only a little bit of time on my professional society. You don't need to be super involved, let alone involved at all, in all of these organizations. It's more important that you perform well in the organizations you are passionate about and that they supplement your academic achievement. You might be extremely passionate about your role-playing or fashion club, but how much value do those clubs really add to your career (assuming you aren't an actor or fashion major)?

Speaking of academics, your ECs should never supersede your academic endeavors. If you find your academic achievement slipping, take a step back and see where you can dial back your involvement. Simply explain to your organizations that you have to focus on school; that should be sufficient. Remember: All of this effort will feel worthless if you don't ultimately get a degree.

After prioritizing your ECs and building your T, it's important to document everything you do for those organizations. From attending meetings to planning events to guest speaking, the more detailed you outline your participation, the easier it will be to translate your involvement into marketable skills. For my current professional role, I have a spreadsheet where I list every task I do, the date completed, a person to verify my participation, and a link to documentation if applicable. I'd suggest doing the same for each of your ECs. It's a bit of work, but it will ultimately make building your career package easier.

Looking Ahead

More than likely you will have a performance review in your professional role. Having a detailed list of your accomplishments will make it easier for you to present a comprehensive package of your work and achievements, and might even result in a larger bonus.

With all of your experiences documented, you can begin aggregating your tasks based on three areas: functions, situations, and tools. These three areas provide adequate coverage of skills you can best market on your résumé, describe in an interview, and ultimately use in the workplace. Next, I describe each of these areas.

Functions

A function is any objective task you have completed or helped complete in a role. Functions are important because they show what you did as well as your ability to get things done and to do those things well. Aside from the tasks you complete for your student employment, functions can include hosting an event, chairing a committee, delivering a speech at a meeting, or any other task you can prepare, execute, and review the results of.

Situations

Unlike functions, which are objective-based, situations consist of the experiences you had handling problems or using soft skills. Situations provide balance to your task-oriented achievements (your functions) by showcasing your ability to act outside your role. These can include time management, conflict resolution, resource allocation, or other areas where you show leadership. For example, one of my situation aggregations was "assisting in strategic planning" as part of my student employment.

Tools

Depending on the field you're aspiring to enter, there might be tools regularly used by the people working in that field. Your experience with these tools (and marketing of that experience) can give you an advantage over your peers. For Computer Science or IT, tools likely include some forms of software specific to the discipline you want to enter. Liberal Arts majors might need experience in WordPress™, and Business majors need to be adept in Microsoft® Excel. It's up to you to figure out which tools are currently used in your industry. When you do, find ways to obtain that experience. It might be obtained through your projects or your academic work, but some organizations will allow you to use a free or discounted version of the tool for academic purposes as long as you have a school email address.

Your involvement in ECs is only as good as how you advertise your involvement. Building a package by aggregating your scores of experiences not only will set you apart as a T-shape individual but will also show potential employers that you have worked to obtain the skills necessary to fulfill the role.

Ask the Experts

Charles "Ghost" Cheatham, Captain at Southwest Airlines

Ghost is one of the most involved and intelligent individuals I have had the pleasure of knowing, and he epitomizes what it means to be successful in a breadth of activities. The advice and anecdotes he shares should serve as an inspiration for you. Fair warning: This section is on the long side; however, I challenge you to read carefully and channel his words in your own life as you begin to leverage your extracurricular experience.

Tell me about yourself, your career path, your current professional role, and what you're involved in outside of work.

When people ask me about myself and what I do, I usually give one of two responses, if not both, depending on the situation:

1. "I am a Jack-of-a-few trades, master of absolutely nothing."
2. "I am in the favor business."

I am considered, by most conventionally accepted standards, a highly qualified and educated expert in many fields, such as real estate, education, aviation operations and training, business, political arenas of analysis and strategic management, ground transportation management, air transportation management, certain fields of medicine, military operations, firearm training and brokering, import/export operations, U.S. tax law, entertainment, investment markets, and other equally bland and broad fields. Although, the truth is, I know very little about anything in this life. Or better stated, there is so much more for me to learn about everything. When the day comes where I think I cannot still learn any more about anything, even in my most trained and skilled areas, I will have failed miserably.

So, to answer your question about me, I am a student of life who never really graduates, but completes a course every now and again, and then enrolls in the next course level. I'm just not a master. Glory be to the Lord for any victories along my path, not me. I'm just an old warrior continually sharpening my sword as well as my use of it. I want to continually improve myself and help make those around me better, all while making the world better.

Now, to the question of *What do I do?* Where the "I'm a master of absolutely nothing" phrase makes people try to get to know a bit more about me, the "favor business" answer usually gets me a more serious question in response from people wondering what this really means. This, in turn, allows me the perfect opportunity to define myself as a person who values relationships over titles and talents. *Relationships are the key to everything, always. You will be wise to remember this, if nothing else I say here.*

A favor is one person doing something for another, and where that someone might be inspired or compelled to return the favor. It is the key potential value in any worthwhile relationship. That is, the value of caring for others and hoping others care for you.

Of course, for me, once a new acquaintance sees and understands I value and prioritize relationships over other successful aspects of my life, then I can certainly open the door to other mutual benefits of growing the relationship. That is, let them know I can engage them on a professional level with my vocational skills—that is, investment help, transport them somewhere, manage their real estate needs, sell their company for them, help them with their taxes, or whatever else might foster a personal, but potentially professional relationship. And if the business part doesn't materialize, I lose nothing. Each person still has a relationship to foster where one day, I may be of help to that person, and that person to me. In a nutshell, this is my business: the favor business.

I believe it is fair to say that you're a pretty busy guy, yet I also know you to be on top of everything you're involved with. What advice would you give college students looking to be involved in a diverse range of activities and still thrive in them all?

There are three areas that contribute to the success of students' extracurricular activities in this modern era and beyond. I call them "The Three Ts": time management, talent cultivation, and tangible/targeted return.

Time Management

This is not your parents' time management issue. The modern student has a seemingly infinite amount of mind-absorbing distractions that must be navigated to find real benefit from participating in any activity. Many times, these distractions are fueled by the fantastic technologies that were meant to increase efficiency, improve performance, and save time. However, the modern path to time management is full of insidiously common pitfalls. So, first and foremost, fight the temptation to become lured into self-absorbing solo activities that fill your time in a manner away from other human interaction. Game addiction, social media saturation, binge streaming, and so forth, are becoming an epidemic where students drift away from people, not toward others. This inhibits idea sharing, learning about other people's skills, and otherwise facilitating meaningful relationships that actually happen in the real world, not in the mobile device world. Hence, choosing activities that force you out into your campus, church, and community, not into your phone, will be a much better use of your time.

Speaking of time, the math of time itself hasn't changed since your parents were your age when it comes to decision-making. There are still only 24 hours in a day; that's 1440 minutes or 86,400 seconds. When students decide to get involved, they have an endless number of activities to choose from. Choose practically where you can make your limited time count most. Obviously, you could choose too many activities, where even simple participation in each degrades available time for important areas like sleep, appropriate academic preparation, and your other extracurricular activities. Avoid the mistake of filling your schedule with too many activities. Thus, the more pertinent question then becomes which activities to choose. That brings us to the second T.

Talent Cultivation

A very important part of choosing beneficial activities will be determining where talent cultivation will most likely occur. There are no human beings without potential talent. Therefore, the good news is that all of us have some. The bad news is that none of us usually recognize the full God-given talent potential we each have. This is just part of being human. Many of us are tempted to find others with similar talents and talent levels where a safe mediocre or unmotivated approach to actual work or new challenges is accepted and/or encouraged. Mediocrity loves company. To get the most out of your time and choice of any extracurricular activity, you will need to fight this urge. Choose activities where participation will actually challenge you, where others around you will certainly have and display their own talents, and where they will expect you to do the same.

Also select activities where you will be exposed to the real possibility of failure—where, win or lose, you will gain experience, judgment, knowledge, self-esteem, and hopefully, confidence in areas where you needed improvement, or at least some polishing. This approach may seem like overthinking the choice of which extracurricular activities to choose, but it is in fact an opportunity for you to determine what your time investment should produce. This brings us to the third T.

Tangible and/or Targeted Return

In the investment world, everything is based on risk and return. Regardless of the amount of risk one might accept, everyone wants the best return possible. This is no different for the choice of extracurricular activities. Choose something where your chance of a tangible return is likely. How?

Like any investment, you must do at least some research to see whether a healthy return is even possible or, better yet, likely. Many organizations in the modern campus environment struggle to keep new members. Usually, that is more the members' fault than the organization's. This is simply because, due to a lazy approach to familiarizing themselves with the organization, the members didn't really know what they were getting into. Do not choose an activity because it's easy to sign up, it's a close walk, or because someone else said it kind of looked fun or interesting. Don't be the investor who failed to do the prep work, and squandered time and resources for himself and/or his clients as a result. Rather, be the investor who knows the desired return he or she seeks and, with due diligence, finds the choice that at least increases the likelihood of a healthy return. Keep the target (what you want to gain) in sight until you capture it.

If students incorporate these three Ts into any other criteria they plan to use in choosing extracurricular activities, they will have a much better chance of realizing good use of their time, improving their skill set, and gaining something useable and lasting from their association. If students take this approach to choosing where to invest their time, chances of disappointment go way down.

How have you found your extracurricular involvement to have influenced your actual career?

There has been a common thread in my involvement in various organizations and activities all my life. That thread is commitment. Once I decide to get involved with a group or organization, activity, and the like, I'm committed to helping ensure success of the collective goals or desired outcome—or at least making the effort better so it may succeed at some point down the road. Hence, the ability to hone my approach to professional tasks and increase my appetite for higher levels of commitment in my extracurricular activities has influenced me broadly in all aspects of my professional life as well as in my roles in community service. By learning the value and, more importantly, the responsibility that come with truly committing to any group, its associated standards, policies, tasks, outcomes, and so forth, I have been prepared for the challenges in the personal, professional, and service roles in which I have been blessed to serve. *Understanding commitment is key.* My choice of extracurricular activities has given me this.

As a father of college-age children, what advice do you offer on getting a job out of college?

I have seven sons. Each has different interests, personalities, talents, and needs, and cannot be treated the same way in all situations. Be that as it may, I try to instill some universal truths in all my children. I will share one here and the advice that goes with it.

Young people need to understand that there are many doors in life that lead to wonderful opportunities for a multitude of benefits, rewards, adventures, accreditations, certifications, prestige, financial gains, power, privilege, acceptance, and any other worthwhile benefit desired. When you are a child, these doors are as far as the eye can see. We live in a great country, filled with an abundance of pathways and doorways for almost unlimited opportunities. The sky truly is the limit, if even there.

With all this said, here is a universal truth: *In life, you are either opening doors or closing them.* The objective is to have as many doors as possible open for you to choose from at any given time. My advice is always to make decisions knowing the impact on the various doors in your life.

Early on, choices and decisions are made concerning and affecting your life. These decisions are made by parents, guardians, and eventually yourself. Each decision will dictate just how many doors you will have open before you at any given time. It is a simple, but important concept to understand. Doors are generally regarded as good or bad. For my advice to my sons to resonate, they have to understand the cause-and-effect relationship when it comes to opening doors, keeping doors open, or closing doors. To best way illustrate this to children and, ultimately, to young adults is to teach them to view how their personal decisions and their personal approach to their own performance, judgment, work ethic, self-discipline, and behavior all play a role in their own specific number of doors. Then help them form the habit of asking themselves before any decision, simply:

❖ Will this open doors?
❖ Will this keep doors open for now?
❖ Will this close doors?

Let's consider some examples.

❖ *Increase number of doors, open doors, or at least keep doors open.*

Displaying a noble character in school or employment, highlighted by your decision-making, will make you successful in building a good reputation. In turn, this prompts letters of reference and recommendations—opening doors.

❖ *Decrease number of doors or close doors.*

Engaging in poor behavior or criminal behavior hurts your permanent high school or college record, or, worse yet, results in a public criminal record—closing doors.

I'm sure you get the idea. Now, my advice is to create a simple template for decision-making that can also be applied to choices in extracurricular activities. For example, *Will organization "X, Y, or Z" open doors or close doors for me?*

Choose organizations carefully. If you join a service organization that has a solid reputation and proven history, you are probably opening doors. If you choose an extremely violent organization with a history of risky behavior or unlawful activities, your association with this group may be closing doors.

So, because my general advice is to keep doors open where those doors might lead to additional opportunities and even increase the total available doors to you, my condensed advice is simply to try not to close any beneficial doors. Make appropriate decisions that give you the most choices—that is, the most open doors.

Of course, some doors should be closed. When that time comes, it should be you who decides when and how to close them, and on your terms. You don't want doors closed without your blessing or closed in ways beyond your control.

There is an emphasis on leadership and initiative as skill sets in young people. How would you describe being an effective leader in the groups that you are a part of?

Once you have committed to serving a group, leadership will follow if you really want to help the organization. Here is a simple advice list to follow, which will make you an effective and respected leader:

❖ *Invest in your team and teammates.*
Invest your time and resources. If you set this example, I assure you that like-minded members will follow. The old expression "put your money where your mouth is" to illustrate seriousness or commitment has always been a truism. Of course, that can be applied to your time, your reputation, and anything else worthwhile. Investing in others is where leading by example becomes a foreseeable reality with predictable and measurable results.

❖ *Make no apologies for making judgment decisions.*
Do not be afraid to make decisions within whatever authority your position encompasses. No one respects supposed leaders who will not make a decision, or who constantly poll the group for fear of making the wrong decision. On the flip side, most everyone respects a leader who has no problem in making important judgment decisions and can justify them when deemed appropriate, even if those decisions occasionally prove less than perfect after the fact. *Members will stand with a decisive manager, even when mistakes are made, if they believe the leader acted in good faith.*

❖ *Take risks, but not unnecessary risks.*
Leadership in many ways could be defined as risk taking or managing risks. All leaders take risks—risks in their subordinates, risks with assets, risks with time, PR, strategy, training, and more. However, excellent leaders do not accept excessive amounts of unnecessary risk. There is a big difference between effective risk taking and throwing caution to the wind. *The fundamental tenant is*

that the reward must outweigh the risk. Otherwise, it is a bad decision, every time, without exception.

❖ *Encourage ownership.*

I believe the difference between achieving marginal results in any organization versus achieving something really special often comes down to finding ways to encourage ownership by *all* members, or at least the core majority. Once you have empowered all levels of the group to "think like an owner," you will see extraordinary talents emerge from the most average of members. Many "leaders" of a group feel self-induced pressure to take the proverbial ball themselves and drag the rest of the group across the finish line. Thus, they see themselves as the hero in any success gained coming from their effort. Team members simply think that person is a ball hog who doesn't trust the rest of the team. *Empower the average member, and you will not be just a hero, but a hero maker.*

❖ *Present a vision of success and a map of how to get there.*

Many career fields pay huge sums of money to those whom have vision. You have seen it in coaching major sports programs, entertainment fields, elite literary circles, and technology fields, to name a few. However, having vision is not a rare commodity that only a few chosen ones get to have. Any leader can be visionary if he or she is willing to set goals, lay out the groundwork, and effectively communicate how to execute the plan to get to where the defined success is realized. Having vision can also be expressed in simply having faith in your team members, your organization's belief system, or your own dedication to finding a way to get something important done. Further still, vision can be as easy as drawing a map of where a group wants to go, making it understandable so others can follow it, and being there when they need some directions from time to time. Remember, even with a good map (vision), there will be times your group might occasionally get a bit turned around or off track. *However, if there is no map (vision) laid out, the group will always eventually get lost.*

Although this simple list regarding leadership could be greatly expanded to be sure, if followed, most any leader will find success just as it is.

For as much leadership in extracurricular activities that you have, you also have a considerable amount of involvement as just a member. When it's time to just be a follower and not a leader, how do you ensure you are effective in that role?

Some would describe their role in an extracurricular activity as successful only if they were able to be in charge of it or achieve some official title of importance. Sadly, this is the norm in most extracurricular organizations in the modern era of résumé building and square checking. Please understand that I am not against ambition nor attempts to build a portfolio of accomplishments that may serve you in your student career or provide opportunities in a professional career down the road. If you have earned it, it's fine to put the feather in your cap. There is a fine line, however, between taking credit for your service to an organization you care about and believe in versus serving the organization only to get the perceived credit on some document.

To keep the fine line clear, follow this simple rule of thumb: *Only join organizations where you have real interests and want to honestly serve the organization.* To know whether or not you are being honest with yourself, make an agreement with yourself to turn down any nomination for elected or appointed office for a predetermined amount of time. Also, find ways to take the load off your organization's leaders. If you take the time to find ways to support and build up others within the organization, the organizational needs will come into better focus not only for you, but also for other followers. That is, simply put the needs of the group first. Find ways to serve behind the scenes, such as doing tasks no one wants to do but are definitely needed. If you do this, you will not only service the group as a good follower, but also ensure that you will be a much better leader later if your group calls on you to assume a title-oriented role. Anyone can be in charge of telling others what to do. But not everyone can be a good follower. It goes back to the question: Do you really want to make this organization better or yourself better? A good follower, with the correct intent, will achieve both!

What is the most impactful extracurricular experience in your lifetime? What did you learn from that role, and how did it help you become the person you are today?

Ranking my many extracurricular experiences would be difficult because each one has contributed to who I have become or am still becoming. Many activities have helped me tremendously in certain periods of my life, and others were critical in other periods. Many roles and experiences come to mind that were critical in my leadership development. I'll share a few here.

It was an honor to serve as a cadet in the U.S. Air Force Reserve Officer Training Corps (AFROTC) at Louisiana Tech University's Detachment 305. During my time there, this detachment was one of the oldest and most traditional Air Force programs in the nation, having been founded in 1947, the same year as the U.S. Air Force itself. In between my sophomore and junior class years, I was sent to Field Training at McChord Air Force Base in Tacoma, Washington, in hopes of becoming a USAF officer while competing against the very best cadets from around the nation. The course criteria encompassed academics, athletics, military drill, leadership exercises, team building, written essays, and public speaking. During the second half of the 6-week program, I was significantly injured and went from leading the pack in most categories to struggling just to keep up in almost all categories. I missed a lot of classes and participation in both individual and group projects. It was a humbling experience because I had taken my health and abilities somewhat for granted until that time.

You see, when you are competitively leading others, or otherwise considered at the top, the road looks much different because no one is in front of you. Conversely, when at the back of the pack, or otherwise struggling to meet the minimum standards or just pass, you have a clear vantage point and vision of everyone's struggles, even the leaders up ahead of you. When leading, I could not see the struggles of the many. Yet, at that point in my competitive life, I really needed to be more multi-dimensional; I certainly needed to sympathize, empathize, hear, and understand others whom, due to my shallow level of experience, were easy to overlook. For my own development, I needed to see things from both front and rear in most every way; and because of my setback, I finally did.

When I bounced back a week or so later, I was far more appreciative of my opportunities and possessed a better understanding of the folks from all skill sets. I knew right away it had been a setback I really needed and was truly humbled by the shallowness of the previous me. Despite my injury and falling behind in many of the graded categories, by the end of the program I had focused on the bigger picture of applying my skills in a better way. That is, I focused more on helping others, and certainly the team. I was more productive, efficient, and an improved leader overall. I finished #1 in my class.

As part of being selected as the top cadet of my group, I was presented with a full pilot scholarship for the remaining 2 years of my college career, pretty much guaranteeing an opportunity to fly jets in the USAF. Because of this, my standing in the Louisiana Tech AFROTC detachment increased dramatically upon my return, which resulted in my receiving the top cadet corps job opportunities during my junior year. These experiences, in turn, allowed me opportunities to be observed in more important duties where performing well eventually resulted in my being selected as the overall Corp Commander of the Louisiana Tech University AFROTC program.

My time as Corp Commander was an opportunity to command hundreds of my fellow cadets. My hand-picked staff and I made a huge impact with numerous changes to our program's operation. For my efforts, I was selected as a Distinguished Graduate, where I received a Regular Commission into the USAF (equivalent to a Service Academy Graduate). This, in turn, opened a door for a decade of service as a USAF officer and pilot, where I had the privilege of serving my country in 50 countries, having participated in four combat theaters of operation. I am grateful for my participation in this college extracurricular activity, which opened so many doors, including my current position as an Airline Captain for the largest domestic carrier in the United States. Much of this path was possible due to a seemingly insignificant defeat, where struggling with an injury and the resulting enlightenment changed how I would relate to others of all skill sets. *This lesson has served me well throughout my life.*

As much as my participation in the AFROTC program helped develop my leadership skills, I must admit, it was not where I received my best leadership experience when interacting with, and motivating, others. That lesson and experience came from another extracurricular activity—my membership in a college social fraternity.

You see, in a military organization, orders are given by those who rank higher than those receiving orders. As a high school and college cadet, I was solidly competent at taking as well as giving orders, depending on the situation. The problem with this type of leadership is that when you step outside the military environment, it does not usually translate well into the civilian or, I should say, real world. My extracurricular activities in the social fraternity gave me an immediate dose of leadership reality. Interacting with others in task-oriented situations in that environment was not simply a dynamic of taking orders and giving orders, according to those appointed or elected to the various leadership positions.

I observed early in my fraternity participation that many times "orders" were simply laughed at or otherwise disregarded if the members didn't respect the elected or appointed officer or, more importantly, didn't believe in what was being asked of them. The temptation of a military-minded person such as myself was to insist that we follow those members in positions of responsibility. Easily, I could have gone down the road of butting heads with those who might go against the grain, but something important happened. I was blessed to see real leadership unfold before me in different, yet more effective ways than I was accustomed.

In the fraternity world, if you want fellow members to act on anything, you can't simply demand it. Leaders have to justify the effort and illuminate the potential reward for members and the organization alike. The members needed to know their efforts would be appreciated and possibly celebrated for doing something for the greater good. As a cadet, I was the most decorated student (number of awards received). Yet, as a fraternity man, having my brothers give me accolades generally meant more to me. Why? I think because any success I had came from working with others who didn't have to accomplish tasks with me, but wanted to. This is an important lesson for anyone, military or civilian: Titles of authority are needed, but real leadership comes from the ability to motivate those around you to do things out of respect, caring, and buying into the task or project at hand. Let me illustrate with a specific example of my experience as a student in fraternal task management.

My fraternal organization was fairly new compared to other fraternities on our campus; we had been in existence at our university only around 2 years. We were so new, in fact, that our particular fraternity group had not yet been recognized as a permanent chapter within our own international organization, which had itself been in existence almost a century. There was a difficult checklist within a tight and constrained timeline that had to be met to gain the chartered status. Many would-be chapters never made it in the time allowed and were simply closed because the headquarters of these national and international organizations knew it was better to maintain a high standard than to weaken their brand recognition by allowing a marginal organization to flounder and struggle for years and probably eventually die out anyway. Hence, it was a real threat to be closed if you could not meet the standard. This is where I came in.

After being a full member in my fraternity for only a month, our student fraternity president and another respected upperclassman asked to see me. It was a closed-door session where I witnessed true leadership and motivation play out before my very eyes. Despite being new, I was not only treated as an equal in our organization but was also convinced by these other students that although the odds were very much against us, they had tremendous faith in me to get the remaining requirements completed and for our fraternity to gain the coveted chartered status inside of the remaining 6 weeks before our window closed. They were honest in admitting that it would not be easy and that they actually didn't know how I could do it, but they believed I would find a way. They cautioned me that if I accepted this role, it would be a very difficult task where I would need the help of just about every member in one way or another. They then offered me the title of Chartering Chairman, where they dedicated a small amount of financial resources ($1,100) and their undying moral support. By the end of the meeting, I was so honored and motivated that I accepted the position and this undoubtedly huge task.

The responsibility of the Chartering Chairman entailed too much to describe everything here, but generally speaking dealt with massive certification paperwork (e.g., community service, academic achievement); organizing a large formal banquet with national speakers, a high-end menu, a secluded venue, service staff, and more; public relations duties of press releases and invitations to university, state, and community leaders; transportation and lodging supporting the invited speakers and distinguished guests; award certificates, plaques, trophies, and the like; an after-party event; and, oh, by the way, quality entertainment for the evening. I was somewhat naïve, but even so understood that I really needed about 3 to 4 months' time and a budget of about $20,000 to pull this off. However, I had only 6 weeks and $1,100. Or did I really have more?

When reality set in, which happened about 5 seconds after walking out of that meeting where I had accepting the Chartering Chairman position, I knew I would have to use not only my talents, but also the talents of everyone in our group and beyond. To do this took a great deal of negotiating, building relationships, gaining trust, and convincing many, many others to buy into the overall effort. We negotiated donations of the venues, some of the food, equipment, and other needed items. We recruited other members, their families, and friends to help with decorations, table settings, and so forth. We hired entertainment, brokered a deal on group transportation, and secured some nationally recognized leaders within the international organization to come and speak. In the end, we got everything done in time, and the chartering ceremony events were a tremendous success by any measurement. However, it was much more than just that to me.

I was trusted with something precious, and I fought hard to ensure its success. This was more than 30 years ago, and many will say to this day that I was a great leader for this project. The truth is that the real leaders were the other two students in that first closed-door meeting with me where they convinced me it could be done with my help. I will go to my grave never being able to repay those two fellow students for not only the impact they had on the success of our chapter, but also on my personal and professional life for the decades since. This project was early in my fraternal experience, which then inspired me to continue to serve in various volunteer capacities within the same fraternal organization in many ways ever since. The Chartering Chairman project would not be my last large banquet-type production; I have helped with more than 20 banquets throughout my years as an alumnus.

It is important to note that I continued to serve over the years because I was initially led to buy into the importance of the original and fundamental tasks facing our organization, and I was given the support and confidence I needed at that pivotal moment in our chapter's history. This extracurricular activity really helped me and the organization with many other successful volunteer tasks, including my service as the Project Manager for the planning and construction of a $2 million Chapter House and Residence Hall structure a few decades later. That project was completed in 4½ months with very little initial money in the bank to work with. However, that's a story for another time.

The bottom line is that the choices in my extracurricular activities not only have had an impact on me but have also defined who I am now and will continue to influence me as I evolve down the road. The old adage really does ring true: You get out what you put in. In my case, I would say I received more than I gave.

What other advice would you give young people regarding their extracurricular activities?

Three short suggestions for extracurricular activities are *choosing wisely, serving honestly and professionally,* and *committing appropriately.* I'll briefly touch on each suggestion.

Choosing wisely has already been discussed with the Three Ts (time management, talent cultivation, tangible and/or targeted return) and the Opening Doors/Closing Doors concept. I will add just one thing. Your choice to participate in something might change your life. You might be getting ready to meet your future spouse, a lifelong friend, or a mentor. *Sometimes you choose things in life, and sometimes life chooses things for you.*

When serving in any activity, serve honestly. This means simply telling the truth when relating to membership. Do not fall into the trap of accepting more tasks or responsibility in a group just because you don't want to disappoint your friends and fellow members. Doing a poor job because you are spread too thin does not do anyone any favors, especially your organization. It is okay to say you can't take on a certain task right now and to ask for something more manageable. On the flipside, be honest when the organization needs help with a task, and you know deep down there is actually no good reason you can't help. It is tempting to be the person who seems to be too busy all the time to work on meaningful projects within the group but enjoys the status of being in the organization. You will definitely meet this person at some point. Simply put, if you can, then you can and should; and if not, say no. *Honesty is essential to serving any group in a professional manner.*

We have already discussed various aspects of committing appropriately. To sum up this commitment advice, I will just reinforce the idea of deciding early to make whatever extracurricular activity you commit to better by the time you leave. If everyone would just weigh this simple measure against their participation and follow through with effort, participation in any group would almost always be considered a success. There are no groups in my personal and professional life where I left the group worse than I found it. *Simply decide to leave your extracurricular activity in better shape than you found it, and everything else regarding your association will take care of itself.*

Wrap-Up

When I was applying for my first job out of college, I would tell recruiters a brief story (an elevator pitch, as I'll discuss later). I'd walk up to recruiters from highly notable tech companies, introduce myself, and say,

> I promise you that I am not the most technically qualified person you will meet today, and I am proud of that fact. I say this not because I have no technical skills, but because I have sacrificed some effort toward technical knowledge to obtain soft skills that would make me a

more well-rounded employee ready to jump into any role headfirst and succeed.

This little blurb got me two competing offers from two major players in the cyber security space, and a reason to dedicate a whole chapter to expanding your skills through extracurriculars.

Extracurricular involvement adds value to your academic achievement, whether through a professional society, service organization, student employment opportunity, Greek affiliation, or any other group. Shaping your involvement with a T-shape focus and then aggregating your documented expertise into functions, situations, or tools will give you a solid package of your achievements along with some concrete talking points to use when communicating your experience to employers. And, when it's all said and done, maybe send an email to the high school guidance counselor who emphasized the importance of being well-rounded and let the counselor know he or she was right, even if it took you until after high school to fully realize it.

Chapter 3

Communications: The Best Person to Talk About You Is You

A t this point you should be well on your way to earning your degree and gaining a considerable amount of extracurricular experience that you can craft into marketable skills. You should feel pretty good about your achievements thus far, but you need more than that. If you cannot effectively communicate those accomplishments, your good feelings about your achievements are meaningless. In fact, you really aren't the person you should be trying to impress. The people you need to impress when going to college for a career are recruiters and employers.

Glassdoor™, a notable career insights service, reported in a 2017 article that the average recruiter or hiring manager spends around 6 seconds looking at a résumé [15]. That means you have 6 seconds to make a stellar first impression, regardless of the platform you use to reach your recruiter. While the résumé remains the de facto tool for evaluating candidates and getting an overall view of their experience, a high-quality résumé alone is not enough to set yourself apart for the job you want. Your cover letters, email correspondence, and even your LinkedIn profile all are factors in getting your foot in the door with recruiters. I discuss all these forms of professional communications here to help you perfect them to the point that recruiters are contacting you about opportunities rather than your reaching out to them.

Resumes

Your résumé is one of the most important pieces of correspondence you'll create with regard to your career. In the 6 seconds you have to make a favorable first impression with your résumé, the quality of this document can be the difference between the trash or giving you cash. It may not seem fair for a person to define all your hard work and achievement at a glance, but you must remember that the recruiter or hiring manager is not waiting anxiously to review your résumé and application. Your application and the other hundreds, if not thousands, are all vying for the same position, and a recruiter or hiring manager has to go through all of them. The question then becomes how you separate your résumé from those thousands of other candidates.

Let's start with thinking about that 6 seconds of judgment. It's a first passing glance, almost like perusing art in a museum. If a particular piece of art catches your eye, then you go up and look at it further. A résumé is a piece of art that even the most inexperienced artist can create. Just as the late Bob Ross believed that everyone can paint, I believe that everyone can craft an original and impactful résumé simply by keeping some core principles in mind. And like Bob Ross, I promise you that I will not give you a color-by-number approach to résumés. Templates are the color-by-number of résumés, and they lack the originality you need to stand out in a competitive job market. Don't use a template; take the time to build your own résumé.

The style you use on your résumé and the contents thereof should ultimately reflect both your personality and your qualifications. Maybe you prefer Georgia font over Arial. Maybe you put a bigger emphasis on your situational work experience when you were building your package in Chapter 2, so you dedicate a section for that. Maybe you think a headshot is important to put alongside your name. The high-level style of your résumé is comparable to a recruiter seeing you walk up to his or her table at a career fair. Will the recruiter see you in business attire or tattered jeans and an Orange Crush™ T-shirt? When you are finished with your résumé, look at it with a peripheral view and see what impressions you get. Ideally it should be captivating; but if not, ask yourself why and change your style accordingly. After your self-analysis, go to your peer network and ask others to do the same. Your résumé having a high-level professional appearance is the first step in getting past those 6 seconds.

Regardless of how you end up choosing to style your résumé, it is important to eliminate as much white space as possible. Going back to that 6 seconds, a large amount of white space makes your résumé appear empty and suggests that perhaps you either do not have a great deal of meaningful content or you did not take an adequate amount of time to prepare this document. Recruiters and hiring managers may think, "If this person can't take the time to prepare a worthwhile résumé, how will he or she perform in the job?" While you might have good content on your page, your résumé will not pass the 6-second test if it looks empty. Yet, don't just pack your résumé like you're getting a one-page cheat sheet on a test. Like a well-balanced meal, it should leave your reader satisfied but not over or under satiated.

Looking Ahead

While "winging it" can work sometimes in your career, adequate preparation for important presentations and meetings is critical to your success. Polishing slides, making and going over speaking notes, and preparing answers to potential questions are important skills that will make you more successful in your role.

To easily fix the white space problem while also keeping your résumé format visually appealing, use unbordered text boxes. They offer a simple way to place your content in different areas of your page without messing up other areas of your résumé. Furthermore, as you gain more experience and chose to move things around, you can add or remove text boxes rather than having to readjust all the content on the page. Text editors can sometimes feel like a house of cards, where one little shift screws everything up. Text boxes offer a more stable and modular structure to compensate for your text editor.

Original artwork is admired for being just that: original. So, why would you not want your own work to maintain its integrity? That is why you should save the documents you send to employers as PDFs, or portable document format. This is for two very important reasons. First, PDFs ensure that the résumé you create is in fact your own. The PDF format prevents anyone from tampering with the content of your résumé and ensures the integrity of your work. Second, a PDF preserves the format and design of your résumé across the various Internet browsers and platforms your recruiter or hiring manager might use. A PDF is essentially an image of the document; when people open your résumé, they will see an image as you designed it. Other formats, when opened on mobile devices or in preview mode, can appear muddled when not saved as a PDF. To save your résumé as a PDF, select "Save As" and change the file format to PDF. It's a simple adjustment that offers a great deal of benefit. However, do remember to keep the original text file for your own updates as well as for uploading to online applications that pre-populate fields based on your content. PDFs tend to be problematic when auto-extracting information; whereas text boxes are less problematic.

So hopefully you've caught their attention with the professional, original style of your résumé. But that style is worthless if you walk up to a recruiter, shake his or her hand and say, "I'm good at PowerPoint® and people skills!" Rather, you would introduce yourself, explain what you're looking for, and what your qualifications are for the role that you want. This same structure applies when presenting the content on your résumé, and why I like to view résumé content as a quality three-course meal: appetizer, entrée, and dessert.

First is the appetizer. It's the first food to arrive, and it sets the tone for the rest of the meal. Your résumé appetizer is the combination of your name, contact information, and either a personal brand or an objective statement. Your name should be the biggest point on your résumé, as it's the first thing you want recruiters to see. The same way you walk up to someone, shake his or her hand, and say your name, so too should you introduce yourself on your résumé.

As a white male, I realize that I have certain privilege when it comes to my name. Even though there are anti-discrimination laws in hiring, there is bias against names on résumés. A 2017 study by Harvard Business School found that African-American and Asian students who "whiten" their résumé have about a 10–15% higher chance of getting a job[16]. Is it fair? Absolutely not, and frankly it's bullshit. I believe you should be true to yourself, who you are, and where you come from; however, the objective of this book is in part to help you start your career. It is ultimately up to you whether or not you choose to "whiten" your résumé. A reasonable compromise in my opinion is a two-initial abbreviation of your first and middle name. For example, instead of listing my name as "Skyler William King," I would use "S. W. King." Do whatever you're comfortable with; no job is worth sacrificing your personal integrity.

Along with your name should be contact information. This is important in case someone wants to reach out to you about an opportunity. You could be the perfect candidate for a job, but if a hiring manager can't get in touch with you, then you're going to be overlooked for that position. At the very least, include your school email address, phone number, and LinkedIn profile if you have the space. Physical mailing addresses have been left out due to the cost-benefit analysis of putting it on a résumé. For one, physical addresses can be bulky, and you only have so much room to highlight your experience on a single sheet of paper. Physical addresses can also restrict your opportunities to the geographic region of the address due to the potential cost for employers to relocate you. I had a friend who was looking for work in the Denver area, but had his Louisiana address on his résumé and wasn't getting any calls as a result. When he took off the address, he started getting interviews. Including a physical address provides another means for someone to contact you, but it probably won't even be used. If a recruiter or hiring manager needs a mailing address, that person will likely ask for it over the phone or by email.

When choosing between a personal brand or objective statement, it really depends on what kind of job you're looking for and when you're looking for it. A personal brand statement describes you and your skill sets, gives an overview of your experience, and likely some examples of your highest achievements. It is for this reason I do not recommend a personal brand for your college résumé. While you do have marketable experience from your extracurriculars, a personal brand reflects some adept level of professional experience in certain areas, which you cannot get even from an internship. If you do choose to use a personal brand (and as an adult, you're more than entitled to do that if you want), then make sure to keep it concise with a maximum of three sentences, and be sure to reflect your most notable achievements. That being said, I did not develop a personal brand statement until I graduated college and gained some experience. Instead, I used an objective statement during my college career.

An objective statement is a description of what specifically you are looking for in your search. It allows recruiters, within those 6 seconds, to understand clearly what kind of work you want and to determine whether they have a position for you. The key to a good objective statement, as with a personal brand, is conciseness. You want to answer any questions recruiters might have, such as whether you're looking for an internship or full-time job, which industry you are interested in, and why you're looking for that position. For example, my objective statement when looking for a full-time job in cyber security was, "To work at an international corporation or U.S. government agency in the field of information security toward the protection and security of cyberspace in both the public and private sectors." I say what job I want, where I want it, and why I want to do it all in one sentence.

I use "international corporation or U.S. government agency" to keep open all opportunities within the scope of the same résumé. "In the field of information security" says what field I want a job in, because working for a large corporation or agency can offer many different roles. By saying "toward the protection and security of cyberspace," I am briefly expressing passion for the industry I am looking to enter. In finance, it might be "to assist others in achieving their financial goals," or "educating the future leaders of our world" for teachers. Whatever your profession, expressing why you want to do a job aside from making money reflects professionalism as well as gives you a chance to show off those passions you delve into through your ECs.

After the appetizer comes the entrée, which in the case of your résumé is your primary content. This is where you showcase all of your work thus far, both in your academic and extracurricular endeavors (remember that work experience encompasses relevant extracurriculars). The content of your entrée should not overshadow your appetizer, so your diner (the recruiter) does not consume the two out of order. Your name, contact info, and objective statement should be the first thing digested before getting into the main content. That being said, the recruiter will likely look at the entrée at a high level before consuming it. Will the recruiter admire its appearance or send it back to the kitchen (or into the trash)? The answer is up to you and how you organize your education and experience.

Most career centers will advise you to put your education above your other experience. I believe this is true if you do not have work experience applicable to your industry, such as an internship or project. For example, when I applied to my first internship, I listed my education above the other activities in which I was involved. After that internship, I listed my internship experience above my education. The reason goes back to setting yourself apart. The person reviewing your résumé has probably seen dozens of other English majors; but leading with a journalism internship you've completed sets yourself apart from other students like you and puts you in a better position to get an interview.

Once you've settled on the order of your education and experience, next is how you structure the titles and points underneath your *Education* and *Experience* sections. For your education information, there are a few key things to include: your major(s) and, if applicable, minor(s); your expected graduation date; and your GPA. If your GPA is not above a 3.0, don't list it on your résumé. While most companies are moving away from a hard GPA requirement, some do still have a minimum. You do not want your other experience to be diminished because of your perceived academic shortcomings. Also, if you're a part of any special program, such as your school's honors college, ROTC, or are a Presidential Scholar, list those under your education if you have the space.

For job-related experience, your heading should include the title you held ("Something Something Intern"), the company you worked for, and the summer or period of time you worked there. Underneath that is where you can fill in the various functions, situations, and tools you came up with from Chapter 2. Whether you structure those in bullet points or a paragraph is up to you; however, I recommend using bullets. It's much easier to read three bullets than three sentences. Whichever format you choose, be sure that the font is differentiated from your heading, yet still easily readable when a reviewer gets to that section.

For projects, your header should include the title of the project, the group it was completed for (your school, company, or organization), and the month/year it was completed as well as the month/year it was started if the project was 6 months or longer. Again, this is followed by your functions, situations, and tools in bullets or a paragraph, as appropriate. Including projects is good if you chaired a committee or ran an event in one of your professional societies, service organizations, or Greek life. You can also list applicable projects you did in classes. For example, my freshman engineering classes were primarily project-based. Those projects were involved enough to allow me to come up with functions, situations, and tools that made up a whole résumé entry. Including class projects, though, should be a last resort because your peers will likely have the same content on their résumés. If you do include projects, make sure to go into extensive detail.

Another consideration for your entrée is whether to reach back to high school for experience. Career centers tend to advise omitting anything from high school on your résumé, but this notion has exceptions. Your summer lifeguarding job when you were 16 might not be relevant to put on your college résumé; however, maybe you did some bookkeeping for your family's business and now you're an accounting major, or you taught a youth group at your church and now you're an education major. If your high school experiences are relevant to the field/job you're applying to, then you should absolutely put them on your résumé. You're trying to set yourself apart from the rest of the pack, and you should take any advantage you can to do so.

As far as listing your high school education, I'd definitely include your school's name and when you graduated, but nothing else. I advise including your high school only because of a personal experience I had at a career fair during my sophomore year of college. I approached the booth of a highly exclusive government agency, introduced myself, and began discussing opportunities with the recruiter. As it turns out, we both went to the same high school—1,000 miles away from my university. Upon realizing, I gleefully pointed out the name of our alma mater on my résumé. This made the conversation much more personal and resulted in a paid trip to visit the agency and an opportunity to interview for a position. On the off chance that the recruiter you're speaking to went to, or is familiar with, your high school, the conversation becomes more relaxed and you will make yourself more memorable as a result. When that recruiter reviews the pile of résumés received at that event, he or she will recall, "Oh, this is the person from my high school" when yours comes up. It's insignificant at the surface, but can make a lasting impact. One little line could mean the difference between making the short list or ending up in the trash can.

The third course is dessert. This consists of the extra bits of information that just sweeten your résumé and help further set you apart. You've proven how you are qualified for the job based on your education and experience, but your dessert is what should make a recruiter want to have a conversation with you. Dessert includes things like relevant coursework, additional extracurriculars, certifications, awards, honors, skills, and passions. These sections should be briefer than your appetizer and dessert so that your hiring manager does not read them before your entrée. To accomplish this, justify your dessert content to the opposite side of your education and experience or below these sections, and size these sections reasonably smaller.

Relevant Coursework should consist of classes you have taken related to the field you are trying to enter. If you're early in your college career and have not completed many of these classes yet, you can list applicable classes that you are currently taking with an asterisk, and then toward the bottom of your résumé, add "*Currently Enrolled." This is good because it shows that you are gaining experience through your coursework despite not having completed these courses yet. It also opens a conversation with recruiters about the classes, whether you're enjoying them, and what you're learning in them. We will discuss more about these conversations later, but for now I would say that Relevant Coursework is a must-have section in your dessert.

Extracurriculars and *Certifications* are other must-have sections if you haven't included all your extracurriculars in your entrée and if you have certifications that apply to your industry. As we've discussed, ECs are activities that you choose, so they provide insight into what you value in life outside of work. Additionally, certifications show that you've gone the extra mile to accredit your skills and separate yourself from your peers. Both bolster your résumé in meaningful ways and add to your well-roundedness.

Unlike the must-haves, *Skills* and *Passions* are sections that should be listed toward the end of your content. If we're being honest, these sections are more filler than anything, but they do add value and uniqueness to your résumé. For skills, go beyond the typical Microsoft® Office and focus on skills important for the job you want. For example, computer science students might include the programming languages they know. Passions are purely up to you and might include service organizations, discussed earlier, because they reflect the things you care about.

If you still have some room for a last bite, maybe include a QR code to your LinkedIn page. I did this to reference content beyond my résumé, but also to add something fun at the end to set myself apart. If you've taken the initiative to develop your own website, instead point to that from the QR code because that takes objectively more effort to create than a LinkedIn page. Your last bite does not necessarily have to be a QR code; it could be a headshot or a quote that is meaningful to you. It's just a little something to wrap everything up.

While you can edit your résumé to better fit each requisition you submit, it might be a better idea to have two or three different versions that closely match the different jobs for which you are applying. (A job requisition, by the way, is a fancy term for an open position.) For example, let's say you are studying information systems. You might have three different résumés for three different general job types: an analyst role, an IT support role, and a developer role. You may be qualified for all three, but the résumé you show a hiring manager should reflect the skills necessary for the specific role. If you send your "developer" résumé, which has your programming experience and personal projects, when you apply for an "analyst" position that requires log analysis and file system traversal skills, you will likely make a less than favorable impression. For these generic résumés, you can build cover letters that expand on the content of the résumés you send with them.

Résumés are important, but that doesn't mean they have to be intimidating. Think about a piece of art when it comes to your style, and how you want to make a good first impression during those 6 seconds when a recruiter or hiring manager first holds your résumé. Then, think of the three-course meal with regard to your content. The appetizer is your name, contact info, and personal brand or objective statement. Your entrée is your education and experience, but not necessarily in that order, to show your qualifications based on your objective. Finally, dessert is the extra little bits such as your classes, skills, and passions that help set you apart. By the time you're done, you should have a piece of paper that both artist Bob Ross and chef Gordon Ramsay would be proud of.

Cover Letters

While résumés are arguably the most important means of communication during your career hunt, cover letters are a close second. Back before the age of the Internet, cover letters were used to *cover* the other contents of a physical job application when you mailed it to an employer. In the information age, cover letters have become somewhat less important; however, they provide a personal touch to your application, and some employers still require them. Whether you have personally interacted with a recruiter or hiring manager before or your online submission is the first contact you have, a cover letter allows you to "speak" to the person in charge of the requisition either in the form of a follow-up or a first touch, depending on the circumstances of your application.

Like your résumé, your cover letter can be constructed with a three-course meal approach to how you present your information. First in your appetizer is your heading, including your name and contact information. Again, this should be the first thing that catches the eye of the reader so that person knows who you are and how to get back to you. Ideally, you have a consistent heading across all of your correspondence, including your résumé, cover letters, emails, and so forth. Your heading might simply be your name left-justified, your contact info right-justi-fied, and a line underneath; however, you can make format it as elaborately or simplistically as you like.

Like any other letter you would write, the appetizer in your cover letter should start with a professional greeting. If you have been working directly with a recruiter or hiring manager, address that person by name in the greeting. If you are responding to a job posting, then default to "To Whom It May Concern."

The entree of your cover letter should do three things: express excitement to work for the company, highlight the rele-vant experience on your résumé, and demonstrate your ability to write professionally. Ideally, your résumé is curated to the skills you need for the job to which you are applying. Your next step should be to comb through all information available to you about the company that you're applying to, such as its website, annual reports, recent news stories, Glassdoor information, LinkedIn, and any other credible source. This information enables you to include in your cover letter positive references to the company in the news cycle, expressions of excitement to help execute mis-sions reflected in annual reports, and willingness to be a part of a strong culture identified on forums by current employees. What you choose to focus on is up to you, but enthusiasm to work with the company should come before the role itself. The role is important, but the company is ultimately the one that is offering you the job. That being said, you might find value in different aspects of companies. For example, let's say you are trying to work in sales for one of the big four telecommunications com-panies (we'll call them Blue, Red, Yellow, and Pink), and you apply to all four. Of the four, maybe you like Blue's benefits, but prefer Pink's corporate culture. Only you can decide what you like about each company, and it is up to you to express those positives in your letter.

Next, you should look carefully at the description of the job. What are the highest priority requirements the company is looking for in the role, and what experiences do you have on your résumé that can support those requirements? This section in your cover letter should highlight those experiences you have, explaining how they qualify you for the role. To make this easier, you can create a matrix comparing the requirements to your experience so that you can visually see how they match up. You'll have two values, each to be given a rating between 1 and 5. One value will weigh the priority of the requirement (5 being the highest) and another will weigh how qualified you feel you are to fulfill that requirement (5 being the most qualified). Multiply the numbers for each requirement, and the highest numbers should be featured in your cover letter. If you find that you do not have at least a 3 for your qualifications with regard to the top three requirements, you should try to build skills in those areas. The better prepared you are for the role, the better your chances to receive it.

Your dessert in this case is simply a closing, requesting a follow-up and a wish to speak with them soon. My go-to tends to be, "I hope this content is suitable to your needs; however, if there is any additional information I can provide, please let me know and I will get it to you promptly. Otherwise, I thank you for your time and look forward to hearing from you soon." This puts the ball fully in the recipient's court and opens up the door for more conversations. Furthermore, your cordiality leaves a good taste in their mouth, as all desserts should.

Throughout the cover letter, it is important to maintain the highest level of grammatical accuracy and professionalism. Think of the way you would speak to a recruiter at a career fair or a hiring manager during an interview, and then create your cover letter as a written version of that same conversation. Your cover letter should be as well-groomed as you would be for those conversations—free from grammatical errors and passing the 6-seconds test. Remember: Your application may be considered among those of 100 other individuals applying for the same job. Anything short of perfection could eliminate your chances of competing for the position. Take the time to clean up your cover letter just as you would clean yourself up for an interview (not literally though . . . nobody likes soggy paper).

Email

In today's tech world, email is king of online business communications. Statista estimated that more than 281 billion emails were sent and received per day in 2018, a figure that is projected to increase by more than 66 billion in the next 4 years[17]. However, crafting good email messages is a skill that is difficult to master: balancing the cordiality owed to any piece of mail—electronic or otherwise—while adapting to the fast-paced agility required in the modern working world. Email is truly an art form, but you don't need to be Michelangelo to figure it out. Next, I discuss the different email messages you will likely send in your professional career as well as the structure of each. Note that the same approaches apply to direct messaging in platforms such as LinkedIn.

In general, email messages can be split into two categories: Initiation and Reply. The two require different formulations for how you construct them. While this may seem like common-sense, the content you include in an Initiation is what you want to convey, whereas a Reply requires an appropriate response. Furthermore, you must consider the audience of the email for each type. Is this email an Initiation to a recruiter you met at a recent career event, or is it to a hiring manager you have never met before? Are you replying to the VP of your organization or answering a quick question from a coworker? Each of these email messages will take a very different shape, and it is up to you to conduct your email behavior based on a balance of the circumstances and your personal writing style.

As alluded to earlier, an Initiation email can take several different forms, but in general encompasses any type of communication where you are starting contact with the recipient(s). This may include a first-touch communication with a hiring manager, follow-up communication with a recruiter you met at career fair, or summarization of topics from a team meeting or event. Initiation emails are generally more difficult to write because *you* are the one driving the conversation, and with that comes the challenge of conveying your point while also keeping the attention of your audience. That is why Initiation emails need to be BRIEF: Bottom-Line-Up-Front, Readable, Informative, Elicit Response, and Finish Appropriately.

- ❖ **Bottom-Line-Up-Front (BLUF)** Initiation emails need a descriptive subject that summarizes the contents of the email. Saying "Hey There" in a subject line not only looks unprofessional, but also does not have any significant meaning to the recipient. In contrast, a subject like "Introduction by Joe Smith Regarding Job Requisition

23791" conveys who you are and what you are emailing about in less than 10 words. In addition to a descriptive subject, it is important that you include a BLUF at the beginning of your email in case your email, for whatever reason, has to be longer than recommended in the second point in the BRIEF format. This should simply be a sentence or two summarizing the contents of your email.

❖ **Readable** In the context of email, readability refers to how quickly your recipient can digest the information you're attempting to convey. A BBC article reported the average attention span to be 8 seconds in 2017, which is 4 seconds shorter than it was in 2000[18]. To drive your point in those 8 seconds, be sure your email messages can be read in about 6–8 seconds. If you can't contain the information to that length, then be sure to break up the content into 1–2-sentence blocks so that it is easily digestible.

❖ **Informative** Include as much information as you can within the readable format. This can mean sending screenshots if referring to a technical problem with the application service or attaching your résumé and cover letter if applying for a job. Include the who, what, when, where, and why in the text of your email. Giving your recipient as much information as possible (while still being readable) allows that person to make an informed response.

❖ **Elicit Response** After crafting a readable and informative email, it is important to tell the recipient what response you would like to your message. You want feedback beyond a read receipt, especially when inquiring about jobs. You might ask simply for a reply to ensure receipt of your message or make a more specific request. My typical go-to is, "Please let me know if I can provide any additional information," but yours might be to set up an interview or request some time to discuss further details. This should be the last sentence of your email prior to your conclusion.

❖ **Finish Appropriately** Once your content is completed, you need to finish up quickly and cordially. Use a phrase like "Sincerely" or "Kind Regards" followed by your name and contact information to properly conclude your email. Configuring an email signature will help with this, and ensure that your name, address, phone number, and email always show up at the end of every email you send.

Once you have sent your email, best practice is to wait up to 1 week for a reply depending on the nature of the email (if it is a pressing matter, make sure to add the urgency to your BLUF). With regard to determining urgency, consider the timeline of events that are contingent on a reply. A critical application deadline of 1 week should probably result in a next day follow-up whereas an informal question about a company's internship program should probably be closer to that 1-week timeframe. If you do not get a reply then follow up, ideally as a reply to your previous email so that the information you previously sent is repeated below your new message. This new message should be short and sweet while also requesting whether you should provide any additional information. And whatever you do, don't be the person who adds "1/99" to your subject line and sends incremental email messages every 15 minutes until receiving a reply (yes, this actually happened).

On the other side of the coin, Reply emails take four different approaches depending on whether you are directly addressed, meaning your name is directly mentioned, as opposed to CC'd (courtesy copied) or a recipient as part of a mass email list, as well as whether or not there is meaningful information. Your type of reply can be determined using the matrix shown here.

	Lack of Meaningful Info	Meaningful Info
Directly addressed	Ask for information needed to make a meaningful reply.	Construct a meaningful reply based on request in sender's email.
Indirectly addressed	DELETE because it bears no significance to you.	Thank the sender for the message and make use of the info as needed.

Of course, use your best judgment in how to reply and maintain an appropriate level of cordiality. If you are making a direct reply based on sufficient info, be sure to follow the BRIEF format, where the only variation is eliciting information if needed for clarification. For all these types of replies, make sure to complete them in a timely manner. You wouldn't want to wait on others to reply to your email messages, so don't be that person to somebody else.

Looking Ahead

A recent CNBC article reported that about 70% of people world-wide work remotely at least 1 day per week[19]. To make up for the lack of in-office communication resulting from remote work, it is critical that your email abilities be sharp. You need to be able to perform well and effectively communicate in an increasingly location-agnostic working world.

It is never too early to start applying these good email practices. In fact, the more you get into the habit of using these tactics now, the easier they will be to apply when you begin your internship and job hunt. Use them whenever you have to email a professor, a colleague in your classes, or peers in an extracurricular activity. You might even turn to your network/team and set up a mock email chain. That way, you can all practice and give one another feedback. Practice makes perfect, and hopefully your etiquette will be contagious for all those you email later on so that everyone can be a Michelangelo of their own communications.

LinkedIn

Since the dawn of Facebook®, social media has become an inescapable force in the way the modern world stays connected. According to a 2018 Pew Research survey, 88% of American adults between the ages 18 and 29 use some form of social media, and that number is 78% and 64% for American adults ages 30–49 and 50–64, respectively[20]. Statistically speaking, you probably use (or have used) Facebook®, Instagram®, Twitter®, or Snapchat®; you might be an active user on all of these platforms. Social media is a powerful tool, which is why it is no surprise that a platform was created for working professionals to connect and expand their respective networks: LinkedIn.

I was 16 when I first heard about LinkedIn. I was working as a lifeguard at a suburban, residential pool where I made a point to socialize with the patrons as a means of providing the best customer service I could. On a slow day, one of the patrons and I were talking, and she was telling me about the work she was doing and the level of success she was having so early in her life. I asked for any advice she would give a kid my age, and the one thing that stuck out to me was to get a LinkedIn profile. I went home and set up a profile, and that would turn out to be some of the greatest career advice I would receive in my young life. I obtained my third summer internship and first full-time job from recruiters who reached out to me on LinkedIn, and a number of my friends have had interviews and job offers through LinkedIn recruiting as well.

LinkedIn is a powerful tool, and its power is only increasing. The same Pew survey found that about one in every four adults in the United States uses LinkedIn[21]. Globally, LinkedIn boasts approximately 590 million users, 44% of which are considered active on a monthly basis. Coincidentally, 44% of LinkedIn users earn more than $75,000 a year. Forty million users are students or recent graduates[22], and you should be one of them as well if you are not already. Whether you're asking yourself "Where do I start?" or you're a seasoned professional, hopefully you'll have an All-Star profile and recruiters will be hitting you with messages before you know it.

Fortunately for you, a majority of work for your profile should already be done. The primary content of your LinkedIn profile should resemble your résumé in that it contains your experience and your education. Take the time to properly format all the content from your résumé into your LinkedIn profile so that it looks clean and professional. Be sure to check your bullet points, because those characters do not tend to copy from word processors to LinkedIn very well, and PDFs in this case are especially troublesome.

LinkedIn also has a series of sections for information from the "dessert" section of your résumé. Again, these can be invaluable to set yourself apart from the competition. Unlike a résumé that gives you 6 seconds to make an impression, your LinkedIn profile invites a recruiter to spend longer perusing your content, in a similar way you might peruse an old friend's Facebook profile. Take the time to add your accomplishments, volunteer activity, skills, certifications, causes, and any other sections you think add value to your profile.

Your LinkedIn profile is given a default page name. This is usually linkedin.com/ followed by an indiscernible string of letters and numbers that usually starts with your first and last name. However, you have the option to change it, and you should. That way, you can add your profile's URL to your résumé or business card, so that it is simpler to copy than the default. To change your LinkedIn profile URL, go to your profile and select "Edit public profile & URL" in the top-right of your screen. On the next screen, click the pencil under "Edit URL" in the top-right and change your URL to something recognizable, preferably just your first and last name, if possible.

Once you've built your profile, add individuals you know to your network. These could be your coursework peers, your professors, coworkers, or even the parents of people you knew from your childhood. In particular, connecting with individuals in higher levels of management can be valuable to you, as well as gives you a way to see their career path and how you might be able to reach their position one day.

Personally, I don't make an effort to connect with anyone I have not met or worked with before I receive the connection request. You will likely get connections from individuals who are obsessed with expanding their network, who want to add you just to have the connection. I prefer to limit my network. If I reach out to someone or like someone's post, I want them to say "Oh yeah, it's Skyler" as opposed to "Who's that?" In the event that you do want to connect with somebody you have not met before in person, add a personal message expressing why you wish to connect. That will stand out in a sea of impersonal connection requests and perhaps make that connection more meaningful.

Looking Ahead

Expanding your network is important, but sometimes it can be uncomfortable to make that first communication with a peer (I know I have personally struggled with this). In general, I believe that people are good and respond well to kindness. When in the working world, it is important to expand your knowledge and thinking beyond your cubicle and your team. Reach out to someone in a different organization and get lunch. You might be surprised by what you learn.

LinkedIn also has user communities much like those I discussed in Chapter 2, "Extracurriculars." Joining these groups can help expand your network to people you share common areas of interest with, including high school, Greek affiliation, industry, service interests, companies you've worked for, and more.

One of the major differences between LinkedIn and your résumé is the Skills section. If you put "team leadership" and "effective communication" on your résumé, that alone might not carry much weight, because most people will have the same thing. LinkedIn adds a capability to have people in your network endorse you for your skills. The more endorsements you have, the more reputable your skills will appear, especially if those endorsements come from successful people in their own right. The ability to get endorsements goes back to the importance of performing well in your academic and extracurricular activities as well as being a contributor to the teams you're a part of, because there might be a time when you want to reach out to your peers and professors and ask for skills endorsements. Your contributions to those activities correlate to how willing these individuals are to give you an endorsement.

Similar to its Skills section, LinkedIn has a Recommendations section. This is exactly like it sounds: an area where your connections can write a review about your work. While your peers can endorse you for your Skills, I'd recommend (no pun intended) saving the Recommendations section for those higher-level connections where a review might be more meaningful. These could include the professors you've connected with, managers you've worked for in a job, or others who can attest to your work ethic and capability to perform. In general, asking for a recommendation should be done in person; however, if you must email the person, then be sure to follow the BRIEF methodology.

With your profile on LinkedIn and your network well-populated, you can move into being an active member. Congratulating members in your network on promotions or wishing them Happy Birthday in a personalized note may seem mundane, but think of how you feel when somebody does the same for you. Spreading kindness leaves a favorable impression on people and will indirectly help advance your career. Beyond that, commenting on posts related to your industry as well as authoring your own will drive you further into being a thought leader in your industry, and your public knowledge will leave a favorable impression on those screening your profile. Posting shows that you are not only knowledgeable about the area you work in (or are trying to work in), but also shows a recruiter that you are a disseminator of knowledge, which has become an increasingly appealing trait in workers.

I would be remiss if I did not mention LinkedIn Premium. LinkedIn Premium is a paid service offered by LinkedIn to help you improve the metrics on who views your profile so that you can tweak your applications, among other added benefits. I personally have never used it, but I know others that have found value in it. LinkedIn generally offers a one-month free trial, so you can try it out if you're interested and see whether you like it. That being said, LinkedIn Premium is not necessary to having a successful profile. Your accomplishments and attention to detail will take care of that.

I cannot guarantee you will experience the same level of success from LinkedIn that my friends and I have had; however, based on the data presented earlier in this section, it is ultimately worth your while to take the time to create a quality profile. Doing so will do nothing but help your profile stand out among the other 40 million students and recent graduates, and will put you in an excellent position when it comes time to apply for jobs.

Ask the Experts

Mrs. Christine Strebeck, Lecturer in Technical Communications at Louisiana Tech University

I had Mrs. Strebeck for two courses during my undergraduate career: Technical Writing and Technical Presentations. These were two of my favorite classes in college, and that was primarily due to the straightforward, commonsense approach Mrs. Strebeck took to teaching. Everything in the courses was targeted to what matters in the real world, not your academic life, and I know her words will help you especially as you begin to prepare your résumé(s) and cover letter(s).

Tell me about yourself, your career path, and your current role.

I am a proud child of the Liberal Arts; I have a B.A. from LSU and an M.A. from Louisiana Tech. In between those two degrees, I spent most of my time in Human Resources. I was first hired to write proposals for a healthcare consulting firm, and then became an interviewer at the corporate headquarters of a multistate retail company. I was an interviewer, recruiter, trainer, and HR director in both retail and healthcare. At one point, my husband took a job at Louisiana Tech, giving me the opportunity to pursue a master's degree in English—a long-term goal of mine. In the subsequent years, I have taught writing, specifically Technical Writing and Technical Presentation skills. The best part of my profession is the students; I want to help them get ready for the real world and enjoy sharing my passion for effective communication with them.

You've been in the position where you prescreen résumés and cover letters for employment. Can you reveal in gen-

eral what that process looks like? What misconceptions are there about how initial communications, such as résumés and cover letters, are reviewed?

Screening of résumés happens fast, and if a company uses a screening program, it happens really fast. Programs screen for key words, and résumés without the right key words are ignored. For that process, it is vital that you include in your résumé as many of the characteristics as possible that the company has described in the job posting and that you use the company's vocabulary.

Screening résumés by hand means looking for bright-line requirements (e.g., certain majors, GPA, internships) that allow quick Yes/No decisions. This may take 5–10 seconds each. No one has the time to carefully read every cover letter and résumé. Easy red flags include grammatical or spelling errors of any kind, too many jobs in too short of a time period, a general lack of information that made me wonder what you did with all your free time, and absence of any information about the basic requirements for the job.

After an initial pass (I put résumés in Yes/No/Maybe piles to make myself feel better, but I never looked at the No's or Maybe's again), I would go through the Yes pile more thoroughly, spending maybe 1–2 minutes each, but again with the intent of elimination. At this level I was looking for education, skills, and experiences that matched the job and the company.

A résumé needs to be well designed so that critical information is easy to access. This is where effective design of headings and subheadings, effective use of white space, and content that is specific about what you know are important. Experienced HR professionals know what works for their company.

The goal was to identify the top three to six résumés and then start reading closely, putting together the person on the page in front of me as a coherent whole. The more I could ascertain about the kind of person and employee I was reading about, the better I liked it. I finally got down to 3–6 to call for initial phone screening interviews. At that point the paperwork finally begins to take a backseat to the human. Fundamentally, screening assumes there are only a few close matches; I wanted to find the best match for the job as fast as possible by weeding out the others as fast as possible. Harsh, but true.

As someone who has worked in both industry and education, what have you found to be the biggest differences between the two realms? What should college students do now to mitigate these gaps?

First, school is mostly a solitary working environment. You test alone, mostly prepare work alone, and are evaluated individually regardless of the performance of others. Real work is collaborative; your success is intricately tied to the success of the group. Even if you work for yourself, you involve and depend on the quality of the work of others.

Second, in education you have to please only your teacher—an audience of one who knows more than you do about your subject. In the working world, you have layers of bosses, clients (customers), and colleagues that must come together to achieve positive outcomes.

You must be audience-oriented to be successful. As a student you should seek opportunities to work on teams, to volunteer in group settings, to be a part of and lead student organizations. You want to be able to demonstrate that you can move and contribute effectively in a group environment and not just by yourself.

In your experiences as both an HR representative and an educator in career communications, including résumés and cover letters, what would you say are the biggest mistakes people make on these pieces of documentation? How would you suggest mitigating them?

Don't use a résumé template. It looks lazy and canned. Create a résumé that reflects who you are in both content and design, and then replicate that design on all your professional communications.

Try to include both what you have done and how well or successful you were in the effort. Don't just tell me that you have leadership skills; tell me when and where, and then what you accomplished in that leadership role? What did you add to the organization while you were the leader? What did you learn from that experience? Don't be afraid to use a few lines of narrative content (as opposed to the ubiquitous résumé bulleted list) to explain what you did. Let me hear the passion and enthusiasm you have your field. Proofread your résumé and get it right. What does it say about you if you can't get a single sheet of paper error free?

In contrast, what things do you look for in a quality résumé, and what common trends have you seen in résumés from quality candidates?

I tell my students that my goal in content and design of a résumé is that when I finish reading your résumé, I don't just want to interview you; I want to have lunch with you because you sound interesting and authentic.

Your content should definitely address your education and experience (paid and unpaid count), but I also want to see some personal information (Skyler's "dessert"). I am hiring the whole person, so getting a feel for who you are is helpful. Interests outside of your profession, perhaps small personal goals, even a personal mission statement, can round out the picture. Accomplishments that suggest what you are capable of—Eagle Scout, athletic accomplishments that took years of practice, participation on a state or national level in an organization, volunteer work you are passionate about—are the things that separate you from everyone else with your major and GPA and make you sound interesting.

Structurally, a résumé should be 1–2 pages and very easy to scan for information based on the application of basic design principles like contrast, repetition, alignment, proximity, and balance. These concepts are easy to look up on the Internet if they are not familiar.

As an educator of those who will become the modern workforce, you probably often get questions about having no experience to fill a role requiring 2–3 years of experience. What advice do you give those students?

Think about what the employer needs from those 2–3 years of experience? The employer wants the ability to show up; work both in a team and independently; meet deadlines; use certain tools or software; and plan, organize, and execute tasks. Talk to people in the business; ask what they do. Figure this out.

Then help the interviewer see how the experience that you do have has prepared you for these things. Just because you didn't get a paycheck doesn't mean you don't have experience.

What roles and responsibilities have you had that define the kind of employee you will be? If you aren't sure, ask someone who has watched you work (e.g., a teacher, faculty advisor, or even a neighbor) what kind of worker you are? Consider all the opportunities you have had in school and outside that have shaped you. Then describe what you did and what those experiences taught you.

Keeping with the theme of the modern workforce, applications have also moved increasingly digital with little to no human interaction prior to the first interview. How do you suggest effectively standing out from the crowd in an increasingly digital world?

That's a tough one if you are referring to the digitalization of the selection process. Just getting the first phone call requires a carefully constructed, scannable résumé. Remember to include key terms, as I discussed earlier. Do research on résumés of successful people in your field. What are they including in their information? How do their résumés look? Find one you like and create your own. Failing to have a professional looking résumé that you created and can adapt is inexcusable.

Participate wisely in social media. Currently, having a well-crafted LinkedIn profile is necessary. Clean up your other social media accounts; employers are looking.

Many companies are using layers of phone then video interviewing where you have to tape yourself talking with no conversational feedback. This requires practice and well-crafted answers that you can deliver easily. I recommend finding a list of "Top 10 Interview Questions" and then writing out your answers. Practice delivering those answers, video yourself with your phone, then watch the video (it is painful, but necessary to watch yourself!). Then when you have to answer under pressure, face-to-face, on the phone, or on videotape, you can do so.

What other advice would you give to students as they prepare their résumés and cover letters?

I am a big fan of personalization of the résumé, cover letter, and thank-you notes and emails. A careful and quick follow-up shows your attention to detail. Make job application materials that you can easily adapt to different jobs, and then keep up with who you sent what. If someone calls, you want to be able to access what you sent.

While you are in college, look for opportunities to participate outside of the classroom in experiences that help make you a well-rounded, well-informed person. You won't work in a vacuum, so don't live in one. Even if having a 4.0 is the most critical factor in your future, there will be others who have that too. What makes you more interesting than everyone else who has your degree and your grades? Find some of those things, do them well, and document what you did and learned. Then capture that experience on your résumé.

Jennifer Humphrey, Director of Network Development at UNITE US

Jenn is a good family friend of mine who has had tremendous success in her career thus far. Her career path is far from conventional, and it is proof that your major in college does not have to define your career. As you read about how Jenn talks about sales, think about how it relates to selling yourself for the job(s) that you want, especially with regard to your emails and LinkedIn.

Tell me a little about yourself, your career path, and what you do in your current role.

I currently serve as the Director of Network Development for a Veteran-owned startup out of New York City. We are a technology provider that addresses the social determinants of health by connecting healthcare, behavioral health, governments, payers, and social service providers in a collaborative environment to track patients and clients in real time, and, importantly, provide structured data on outcomes. In this role, I am responsible for business development (outside sales). I drum up new leads through prospecting, handle all presentations and negotiations, and ultimately nurture relationships into tangible contracts and revenue for my company. There is a lot of travel involved in this type of role, which is exciting because I am the tip of the spear for the company in ensuring that our pipeline and book of business is successful to grow the company rapidly.

My career path from a young age, due to personal reasons, was always to be a doctor—specifically, a pediatric oncologist. I did all of the right steps in school to get there; I was a Biology major, completed both bench and clinical research internships, and even got published in an academic medical journal as a result of my internship at the National Institutes of Health. I worked extremely hard to meet that goal and was one of the few premed students accepted to medical school while still in college. However, once there, I quickly realized it was not the career and lifestyle for me, and I felt that I truly didn't belong in a practitioner profession. Political changes to healthcare at the time made the field extremely volatile; the rate of physician burnout and suicide was widely reported; and I was frankly miserable.

After 2 years, I made the hardest decision of my life at that time: to withdraw from medical school. I had no idea what I would do because I hadn't considered a single other career path since I was 13 years old, but I knew I couldn't continue in my current direction. After a few months' hiatus, I made a list of "strengths and weaknesses," including things I enjoyed doing and things I would never want to do. My strengths all seemed to center around my competitive nature, desire to not only succeed but to win, and to be financially secure. I realized that sales fit those elements of my personality to a T. You have to be a self-starter, you have to have a strong emotional quotient to deal with constant rejection—there are hundreds of no's before you get a yes, and you have to be able to manage multiple deals at one time. Also, the fact that commission dollars are directly tied to performance didn't hurt either.

I knew I was comfortable within the healthcare space, and I initially set out to find a job in medical device sales. However, I began my job search in 2012 when opportunities like this were at an all-time low, particularly for recent graduates. To add insult to injury, I quickly realized that despite my résumé full of academic successes, the companies I was interested in were accepting only candidates with business backgrounds. I was devastated with the realization that, for the first time, my numbers simply didn't speak for themselves. However, as in anything, persistence is key. I continued to diligently search, refine, and gear my résumé and cover letter to each application. Eventually—8 months later—I landed a job as an Account Executive (inside sales) for a medical analytics software company. The pay was far below industry average, but I was desperate, and I knew that it would be a stepping stone to teach me what I needed to know about sales so that I could eventually pivot into a successful outside sales position in healthcare.

I initially expected to stay with that company for a year or two max; however, about a year and a half in, I realized that I had fallen in love with technology sales as opposed to device sales. I was holding formal meetings in board rooms with the CEO (executive), COO (operating), CMO (marketing), CNO (nursing), and so forth of the hospital. It was empowering when I realized that a roomful of grey- and white-haired men making millions of dollars in salary saw a young girl walk into the executive board room, immediately discredited her due to age and appearance, and ended up realizing that she knew more about their organization than they did and was worth their time. I moved up twice within that company, rising to a Territory Manager covering the entire Midwest and West Coast markets.

Eventually the company sold to a larger company, bringing an entirely new management structure and staff. I adored many of my counterparts on the sales team, but the Vice President was extremely misogynistic, and I came to learn that I was being paid about half of the men's salary for doing the exact same work. I know there is a gender wage gap and understood that I was the youngest person and only female on my team, but that disparity was too much to ignore. After negotiations and numerous failed promises, combined with the toxic atmosphere in the organization, I ended up in my current role where I negotiated for more than double my last salary. Years after leaving medical school, I am still in the healthcare field, but truly love the culture of my new company and know that what I'm doing is helping people in need—just in a different way and with a greater reach than I would have achieved as a physician.

Outside of work, I truly love to travel. It is a blessing that I get to do it for a living (though locations are not always glamorous), and I have developed quite a hobby of playing the "points" game—accruing status and points for flights and hotel stays that I can then use for personal travel. Attending Mardi Gras in New Orleans, spa weekends at resorts in Arizona, vacations to the Caribbean, and even a yoga retreat in Costa Rica have all been (mostly) paid for with points I've earned through doing my job (and strategic credit card use).

Because I am always on the go, it is important for me to take time to myself, and yoga is one of the things that challenges me, calms me down, and allows me to disconnect for an hour. In sales, because what I do directly affects how much I make, I have a hard time "shutting down." If an email comes in at 9:00 p.m. from someone in a different time zone, I answer it. It's important to not overwork yourself and to take time for yourself, which yoga helps me do.

I also love live music, and whether it is seeing The Rolling Stones, stumbling upon a dark and smoky jazz bar, or even randomly catching a show at Red Rocks while in Denver, I will never turn down listening to a talented artist doing what he or she loves.

Additionally, I enjoy dining out and I make a point of going to the "local" places in a city to really get a feel for where I am. Why go to a national chain restaurant when you could be eating fish tacos and ceviche from a hole in the wall in San Diego, deep dish pizza in Chicago, bison steaks in Wyoming, Tex-Mex in

San Antonio, or gumbo, étouffée, and fresh oysters in Louisiana? Looking back, it's ironic how my hobbies and what makes me "me" still in many ways tie back to what I do for a living, because I finally love what I do.

You started out in medical school, then transitioned into a career in sales. What would you say were the biggest adjustments you had to make as you made that career pivot?

By far, the biggest adjustment was moving from a strictly clinical, scientific mindset to that of a businessperson. It took a few years to truly understand all of the business vernacular after never taking a business or economics class in my life; and unlike science, where over-explaining yourself is necessary, the most successful people in sales are concise and to the point. It was humbling to realize that I had so much to learn and that a lot of those things simply come with time and practice. Now, I am helping train a new inside-sales representative who transitioned from the military, so he's in the same boat that I was in terms of making a complete career pivot. In sales, so much of your success comes down to personality. You can be taught how to talk about what you're selling, but if you don't have the ability to grab an audience from the get-go and make them like you, you won't succeed.

When hiring new representatives, I look for personality and tenacity, not whether they are experts in the field. One of the best pieces of advice I was given is, "People buy from people they like." While I wholeheartedly stand behind the fact that my company is leading the way in terms of restructuring social service delivery and thereby healthcare as we know it, my passion for our work alone will not translate into dollars. I have to build rapport with my customers. I recently told our new trainee, "Some of your most successful cold calls will never once touch upon what you do." People like to talk about themselves, and if you get someone—even a gatekeeper—to talk about his or her Christmas vacation, kids, pets, dinner, or literally anything personal, then you had a successful call. That was so new to me—I started out wanting to just talk and talk about what my company does and how it will help them achieve success. The best thing I learned was to just shut up and listen.

As a person in sales, I imagine you send and receive a considerable amount of email on a daily basis. What have you found to be the defining characteristics of a well-received email to your clients?

The best emails from a salesperson have a few characteristic points. The first is a well-thought hook, usually a personalized subject line. I now have a technology linked to my email where I can tell whether someone has opened or clicked on an email I sent, and I use that technology (Hubspot®, but there is other free software available that has similar functionality) to hone and adjust my subject lines to get people to actually open my messages. Personalization is also key. Rather than just copying and pasting the exact same email to everyone I are prospecting, I take the extra few seconds to write out a personalized greeting, address someone by name, and reference the exact name of the company.

Brevity is SO important. Nearly every person I'm emailing doesn't sit at his or her desk opening emails all day. These people are on the go, reading from their phone or tablet. If you are writing paragraph after paragraph about who you are and what you do, you will never get a response. Bullet points are my personal favorite technique, as it forces you to be brief and list out the key reasons why you will add value and why they should want to talk to you. These are easily referenced when you get someone on the phone and should give them just enough to leave them wanting more. The point of an email is not to sell your product; it is to get to a next step—whether that is a phone call, a demo, a meeting, or the like. Long drawn-out emails are often not read and will not result in that next step.

The best email ends with a call to action—a soft close, if you will. If it's to set up a conference call, end the email with one sentence saying, "Do you have 5 minutes next week to discuss?"; or even suggest a time or two, such as, "Do you have any time next Wednesday around 3:00 p.m. to connect?" An email sounds so innocuous and simple, but a well-crafted email actually takes a long time to hone. However, like riding a bike, once you get it down, it becomes second nature.

In contrast, what are the biggest mistakes you see in email messages from fellow employees that impede success (without naming names, of course)?

I have seen so many emails from colleagues that I *know* won't be successful, simply because they are so wordy and drawn out. Writing paragraph after paragraph about what you do and the value you will provide to XYZ organization is, frankly, jumping the gun. You just need to hook someone, not close the deal through one email. So many people forget that fact. You can have that ROI (return on investment) conversation later, so an email does not need to go into the specifics. It needs to lead to that ROI conversation. Including too much is overselling and comes off as cheesy and pressured. Nobody wants to buy from the stereotypical used-car salesman who will back you into a corner. I specifically ask for a few minutes—not for a sales pitch, but to ask a question. People want a collaborative, open dialogue with someone they trust and like.

One colleague made a fatal flaw in his emails: He would (obviously) use a thesaurus or right click to select synonyms to make his wording seem fancy. This just came off as superfluous, obnoxious, and unclear, especially when the word didn't mean exactly what he meant it to mean. Be yourself in your emails while being brief. Don't use words you wouldn't use in conversation; otherwise how awkward would it be if you were to actually speak to the person on the phone or in person? Don't oversell, and don't forget to end with a call to action. Otherwise, what's the point?

As a Director of Network Development, what would you suggest to young people who are starting to develop their professional network?

It is amazing how a well-built professional network can continue to feed you for years. Professionalism is key, but so is being genuine and likeable. A little bit of background research when first talking to someone goes a long way. I don't mean stalking a person's Instagram or Facebook page and knowing that the person's dog is a 12-year-old Bichon named Sugar; however, knowing where the person went to school, what he or she majored in, or where the individual is originally from goes a long way in understanding what makes someone tick. For example, I travel to Los Angeles frequently, and on a recent call with a young woman from LA, I specifically asked her about her

favorite restaurants, and we ended up swapping recommendations for 10 minutes. After that seemingly unproductive chat, we
had built rapport, established mutual interests, and I know that
this one person will be a viable contact to introduce me to many
other prospective leads.

Also, never discount someone based on his or her current
position. The gatekeeper is often in that role trying to work his
or her way up the ladder, and establishing a true friendship with
that individual not only can help get time on an executive's cal-
endar, but can help you more than you imagine as you continue
to grow and move up within your own position. Gatekeepers are
often the most viable resource. While they're not the ultimate
decision maker, they decide who gets through to that decision
maker. Never forget that.

Forming strong relationships with colleagues is also a huge
factor in building your own professional network. You never
know who you many need to call on for advice, a reference,
even an introduction; so, don't burn bridges or be too closed
off. Obviously not everyone will be your cup of tea, but a few
colleagues that you can truly trust are indispensable, no matter
where your lives and careers may take you.

You never know who you're sitting next to. Whether at a bar
or restaurant, on a plane, or on the bike next to you in spin class.
Networking can often lead to surprising leads and opportunities.
**How do you use LinkedIn in your role? Are there any
practices that you have found make more of an impact
than others?**

Historically, I have used LinkedIn to connect and stay in
touch with people I'm working with—both people I'm selling to

as well as colleagues. You can learn a lot about people from their LinkedIn profile and posts, and that often gives me just enough background information before jumping on a call to casually reference or bring up a similarity I may have noticed. I also have recently started to post/repost more about my company. While I can't translate it into dollars and cents yet, I think it adds to the presence and validity of my organization.

I am also currently trying to convince my company to purchase LinkedIn Sales Navigator. I tried it out through a free trial and absolutely loved that I could search within my territory for a specific title and then could contact that person directly. I only had a month of trying it out, so I honestly can't speak to its long-term efficacy but hope to have more insight soon.

You have a younger brother that just entered the workforce. What advice did you give him that you would also give to others beginning to enter their career?

In terms of general career advice, I told him to be the first one in and the last one out every day. Yes, you're starting at the bottom of the totem pole, but people are always paying attention. Anything you can do to set yourself apart from the crowd will only help you move up faster. I stressed to him the importance of professionalism around colleagues. Eventually you will make friends you will hang out with on a Saturday night, but you never want to be the drunk recent grad at the holiday party falling over the Christmas tree. Let those relationships grow organically, and again remember that someone is always watching.

I additionally told him how important it is to take time for yourself and not make your job your entire world. Work-life balance is critical, and if you don't start off with the understanding that your time is valuable, it will be extremely difficult to learn it later on once you have even more responsibilities pulling you in different directions.

Never be afraid to negotiate. The first offer is never the best, and when starting out always see what more you can get. That comes with knowing your own value and worth, and I think negotiating actually instills more respect from your employer than just taking what you're first offered.

When in doubt, always overdress. T-shirts and jeans were great in college and might even work for some workplaces, but for the most part are not acceptable in a professional environment. Even on casual Fridays, I would still encourage wearing a collared shirt. For women, never wear anything too tight, short, or low cut. How you dress impacts how your colleagues view you, and you don't want to lose respect for something that could have been avoided simply by trying a little harder or having higher regard for the opportunity you've been given.

Your work is an opportunity. It's an opportunity to grow, to find what you like and don't like, to make contacts and friends, to make money, and to gain satisfaction in the same way you'd be proud when you bring home a report card with straight A's. If it's not working for you or the culture becomes toxic, there are other opportunities out there. You just have to go find them. Never stop growing or become complacent—you'll be shocked where you end up if you just keep pushing.

On a personal note, I was honestly shocked that my brother decided to pursue sales, but so proud of the success he has achieved in less than a year with his company.

Wrap-Up

I'm sure you are sick and tired of hearing about the importance of effective communication. Poor communication is unacceptable—from the telephone game when you were in grade school to your significant other not snapchatting you back while you were reading this chapter. Communication is an unavoidable part of our daily lives. The working world is no exception, and if you are not able to convey information about yourself and your experiences effectively through your résumé, cover letter, email correspondence, and LinkedIn profile, then you will likely fall behind in the hiring process.

Think of your team as a gear-based machine, where each team member is one of the cogs. For the machine to work, all the cogs have to have their teeth match up to one another. If one falls out of sync, then the whole machine collapses. Effective communication is the same way in that when one team member fails to communicate effectively, the whole team falls out of sync—causing the need to stop and fix problems rather than complete the objective of the team. Don't be the bad cog and also help ensure that there aren't other bad cogs in your group. Hopefully you'll find yourself and your group working like a well-oiled machine.

Chapter 4

The Hiring Process: Getting the Offer You Want

By this point in your college career, you should be in pretty good shape for getting your two pieces of paper. Your academic affairs are all in order, and your extracurricular portfolio is diverse and meaningful to both yourself and your career. Your résumé, cover letter, and LinkedIn profile are all up-to-date, look great, and sell the best version of yourself. Now it's time to use all your efforts thus far and apply them, specifically to jobs.

The modern hiring process can be tricky to navigate with the assortment of components companies have added over the years to evaluate well-rounded candidates like yourself. You have to be on the top of your game every step of the way to ultimately get that internship or job you want. If your initial application does not have the right key words, then you won't get past the automatic filter. If it doesn't look good, then it might not pass the quick scan by recruiters. If you interview poorly or look disheveled during career fair, then you will likely be passed over for a more put-together individual. Those points should not come as a surprise to you based on the previous chapters in this book, but they're important to remember as you begin competing directly with your peers for the job of your dreams.

The hiring process is also quite variable in both how it runs and who the hiring managers select. No two application processes will be exactly alike, but they all will have similar components, which I will discuss. Even if you think you are the perfect candidate for a position, there is no guarantee that you will ace the hiring process and get the job you want. This is due to the human element of the hiring process; there might be two applicants with nearly identical skills and experience, and the company picks one over the other purely based on a gut feeling or a seemingly arbitrary preference. Does it suck? Sure. But if you've done the work in the previous chapters and continue to push through, then hopefully you'll be the preferred pick. If not, put it behind you and move on to the next target.

Throughout this process, stay positive and be as relaxed as possible. This is the chance for you find out what you really like and where you could potentially end up working. Take the process seriously, but not too seriously. Be yourself, and never try to be something you're not. If you're enjoying the opportunities to interact with people in the working world, then it will reflect positivity in your interviews and help you stay optimistic. You're ready, so let's start getting you a job!

Setting Goals

Before you start responding to job requisitions, you need to figure out what job you want. You should already have some idea what you want based on the considerations covered earlier. Now is the time to determine exactly where you want to end up. Think of what you want from the stages of your career: an ultimate goal, a mid-career goal, and an entry-level goal. Your ultimate goal should represent what kind of position you would ultimately like to achieve in your career (within reason). Not everybody can be the CEO of a Fortune 500 company or President of the United States, but you can have a reach goal of being a regional director for a company or a member of Congress. Maybe your ultimate goal is centered more around responsibilities or perhaps wealth. Your ultimate goal should be where you see yourself at around 15–20 years into your career, and your mid-career goal should be a milestone to reach so that you will be where you need to be to achieve your ultimate goal. Your entry-level goal should be a position that will help you get to that mid-career goal, and it is what you should focus on in the hiring process.

These goals build off each other; they are your path to your ultimate goal and should represent a logical progression. If your ultimate goal is to be a financial director, you probably won't get there if your entry-level goal is to be a cyber security analyst—but a financial analyst role could work. Without the right job progression, you will find that you don't have the necessary skill sets to reach that ultimate goal for your career. While this plan is likely to change over the course of your lifetime, it's still a good idea to have a basic plan in place to guide your path. For example, my ultimate goal is to be a Chief Information Security Officer (CISO) of a major corporation. To get there, I set my mid-level goal to be an information security manager, and consequently opened up my entry-level goal to any opportunity that would give me the breadth of cybersecurity experience I needed to get to that mid-level goal. Will this plan change? Probably so, and yours likely will as well. For now, you have a path in place to help you stay on course; but if another opportunity comes your way, then be sure to take advantage of it if it's a direction that interests you.

Unlike your cover letter, where you put the company ahead of the job, in the hiring process you focus on the job first and the company second. This advice is based on the same strategy you used when selecting a major versus selecting a college: You want to go to the school that will give you the best chances to achieve your goals rather than fit your goals to the school. In this case, you want to go to the best company that will help you excel in your career. Let's say your goal is to become a CPA. Sure, you could start out as a marketing agent for a department store, but wouldn't it be a faster track to start at an accounting firm? The more quality experience you gain in the roles you need to get to your mid-career and ultimate goals, the higher likelihood you will achieve these goals. There are benefits to working at large multinational corporations just like there are benefits to working at a small business. A similar role in any organization will carry out similar functions; it is then up to you to brand yourself well enough to excel beyond that first role.

Your entry-level goal is the second piece of paper you're working toward (your college degree should always be the first). It's the job offer that puts you on a trajectory for success in your career, and it's what will help you achieve your ultimate goal. Entry-level goals should correlate with your résumé's objective statement, and all of your work thus far in your academic and extracurricular affairs will help you get there.

As far as planning these goals, consult your recently established network! Your professors are a good place to start, because they have a doctoral-level understanding of the industry and can help you flesh out your goals based on where you want to go in your career. Your peer team is also good to consult, because your peers are going through the same process as you are and will hopefully give you honest advice on the targets you've set and whether or not you should adjust them. LinkedIn is a fantastic tool to use when determining your goals as well. You can search people currently in roles related to your ultimate goal and see what their career paths looked like. Doing this is useful because it shows you the different roles individuals held along with the number of years it took them to get to the level of your ultimate goal. Especially if you know the people or have a connection of some type, you might even send a couple individuals a personal message asking to meet with them in person and discuss their career path. Most people are eager to talk about their careers with younger people like yourself and may even mentor them to where they want to be. If you're still unsure about your career progression goals, a simple Internet search can go a long way in investigating what jobs you need to get to that ultimate goal.

Doing Your Research

Once you've determined your entry-level goal role, you can begin to find the open requisitions that match this goal. A job requisition is a fancy term for an open position. The position titles might vary between companies and requisitions; however, the roles and responsibilities should be comparable. So read each requisition carefully. Companies have entire Human Resources teams dedicated to crafting these requisitions based on the needs of their business. They know what they are looking for, but it is up to you to show them how and why you fit the role. Generally, the roles and responsibilities are ordered by priority. This means you should apply the résumé and cover letter formatting discussed earlier, placing emphasis on the most important roles and responsibilities accordingly. You wouldn't give a patron at a restaurant an order of fish if the person ordered a steak, so give the recruiters or hiring managers what they are looking for in an employee. Take the time and curate your résumé and cover letter to ensure that the company gets the beautiful porterhouse steak that you and I both know you are.

Some companies have web pages dedicated to student employment. These companies have gotten smarter in recent years and have adopted an internship-to-full-time pipeline strategy where you assimilate with the corporate culture of a company so you can hit the ground running once you graduate. While this does make life easier knowing you have job security in your back pocket, it's not a bad idea to experience different companies while interning. I worked for three different companies during my three summers, and I was able to experience three very distinct corporate environments and teams. This mix allowed me to identify what I liked and what I didn't like in companies, where I wanted to work based both on the company and region, and what it takes to get hired in these companies when applying for jobs my senior year. Ultimately, it is up to you to decide where to apply, but know that you have options beyond the companies where you've interned.

As you begin to search through requisitions, you should also be researching the companies that hold the requisitions (like you did when constructing your cover letters). Not only will this give you more information about the place you may work in the future, but it will also show employers that you care about the potential to work for their company. During your search, you should ask yourself the following questions:

- ❖ What does the company do and how does it do it?
- ❖ What values does the company hold and how do they align with my own?
- ❖ What opportunities are there beyond my internship or entry-level job?
- ❖ How do current employees feel about working there?
- ❖ Has the company made any recent headlines? Are they positive or negative?

Answers to all these questions will give you good insights into the company you're applying to. The Internet is your friend in this search. The company's website, a search engine like Google, and forums such as Glassdoor and LinkedIn should provide you with enough information to answer the questions and reach reasonable conclusions about a company.

Speaking of LinkedIn, this is a powerful resource for finding jobs as well. Not only does LinkedIn curate available job requisitions to your skill sets and interests, but it also provides a platform for recruiters to reach out to you directly if they believe you would be a good fit for a role, either an internship or a full-time role. Being contacted by a recruiter is an ideal scenario; if a recruiter reaches out to you, then you know the company is already interested in speaking with you, and it becomes a matter of performing well in the preliminary interview to move on to the later stages.

I suggest applying to as many positions as possible, but restricting yourself to one or two requisitions per company. As my Opa would say, you want to cast a wide net to get the entry-level position you want; you do not want to appear desperate to work for one particular company. At the same time, you should put a consistent level of effort into every application, interview preparation, and general professionalism for every company you apply to. For one, it is good practice; but it also allows you to make a more lasting impression on those reviewing your applications. Furthermore, recruiters tend to network amongst themselves; so, a particularly unfavorable impression with one hiring manager might get you blacklisted from other companies you apply to. Moreover, you must assume that there are hundreds of other applicants aside from you. If you slack off, even for what you think is a sure thing, then you might find yourself missing out on any job at all.

As you set your goals and research requisitions, as well as the companies offering them, feel confident in knowing that you have worked hard to have the skills you need to work in the entry-level role you want. You've done everything you can to walk the walk and convey that walk in a way that accurately reflects your skill sets. But be careful: All of your efforts and research will be for naught if you slip up during the application and interview processes. In addition, believing you are right for the role before you have it is just as important as it is when you work in that role. Maintain this confidence throughout the hiring process, and you will be on your way to the second piece of paper.

Applying

Now that you have determined the positions and companies you're interested in, it's time to apply. Depending on where you found the requisition, the application can take many different forms. I will review some of the more popular application mediums in this section, but if you have any questions, it is best to reach out to the hiring manager or recruiter responsible for the requisition. Making this contact not only will give you the clarification you need, but also will create a personal connection with the person who will be reviewing your application.

This is a good point to discuss when you should start applying for internships. When I was a freshman in college, I remember being deterred from attending career fairs or applying for internships because of the lack of experience that comes with being a first-year student. Fortunately, I had a good mentor who frankly thought this logic was ridiculous and encouraged me to apply for internships anyway. I ended up with an internship my first summer home from school and got a head start on my peers with regard to my marketable industry experience. Because I lacked experience in the position, I found myself being open-minded to new opportunities and able to be comfortable with learning rather than achieving certain levels of performance. Just because you are a first-year student does not mean you need to wait; going through this process will benefit you even if you don't get an internship your first summer.

Online

As I've said before, most, if not all, applications are moving to a completely digital format. This makes your job as an applicant both easy and difficult. On one hand, you can apply to several jobs within minutes, but on the other hand, you might get stuck reformatting your application for hours to accurately showcase all of your experience. Again, this formatting is very important because you want to paint yourself in the best light possible.

If you have the option, upload your LinkedIn profile or résumé to prebuild your application. This will save you from having to reenter the information, as well as give the hiring manager those additional resources you have worked so diligently on to reflect the best version of yourself. Once you've done that, visit all tabs in the application and ensure that the information is present and formatted as presentably as possible. Carefully check your education and experience, because the designs of résumés sometimes are not picked up by the software and can fail to enter the information accurately or in the manner you want.

If your application has the option for a cover letter or letters of recommendation, it is always a good idea to include them, whether required or not. Even though you already have a cover letter prepared, make a point to edit it to fit the company and requisition you are applying for. Your letters of recommendation should come from people that can speak to your work ethic and experience, such as professors, supervisors from other jobs, or extracurricular advisors. You should request these letters in person; however, a phone call will suffice if an in-person meeting is not possible. Give the person adequate time to prepare the letter, about 2 weeks; just 1–2 days' notice is not enough. With enough time to prepare the letter, the person you invited can write you a well-constructed recommendation. Also, this advance notice is respectful of the person's time; after all, the person is doing you a favor. And, of course, make sure the person sends the letter as a PDF so the integrity of the work can be ensured, and send the person a thank-you note after you receive it.

Once you've applied for a position, you should receive a confirmation email verifying that your application was indeed successfully received. In some cases, an email address for the hiring manager responsible for your requisition might be provided. Using the email strategies discussed in Chapter 3, you might send that person an email expressing your excitement about the potential to work for that company and about how you hope to hear back soon regarding an interview. Sending this message shows the hiring manager that you're serious about working for the company and, again, separates you from the pack.

While online applications can be awkward, they are possible to manage. The effort applied to your correspondence thus far should eliminate most of the work, other than minor tweaks and revisions. Be sure to make all needed adjustments; doing so will make a noticeably lasting impression compared to the other applicants.

LinkedIn

Unlike many online applications, LinkedIn's job application portal is efficiently designed. Because the portal is integrated right into the site, applications through LinkedIn pull your entire profile and build your application around it. Employers are likely expecting this prebuilt application because they placed the requisition on the platform in the first place. Add whatever additional information you need (e.g., résumé, curated cover letter, letters of recommendation) and submit the application. Again, if there is a LinkedIn profile attached to the requisition, be sure to send that person a message expressing your excitement to potentially be a part of the team.

Career Fairs

Most colleges and universities have at least one career fair each year. This is a chance for employers to come directly to your school and speak to you about potential internships and full-time roles within their company. These companies make a point of coming to your school for a few reasons, but primarily alumni relations. Because they are familiar with the programs and values instilled during undergraduate study, alumni who love their school want to come back and bring more people from their school to their workplace. Recruiters and hiring managers also recognize the work ethic and talent that comes out of schools based on how their respective alumni are performing in their roles. Unless you already have a signed offer for the full-time job (not internship) you want, you should register for and attend your school's career fairs.

As beneficial as career fairs are, they can also be very intimidating. I remember showing up at my first career fair in a new suit with a handful of résumés in a manila folder and being surrounded by hundreds of other students looking almost identical to myself. From there, I wandered the event hall looking for the companies I wanted to talk to and then stood in line to speak with the recruiter working each booth. Recruiters could see me patiently waiting while they were talking to other individuals. Once I got my turn to talk to them and shake their hand, it all felt like a very rushed conversation. When I walked away, I was feeling that I did not reflect the best version of myself. Sadly, this might be the way it is. But these circumstances do not mean you will have the same experience as I did. In fact, with the right preparation, you can do far better than I did.

The first step in preparing for a career fair is to get the right look. While it's true that most workplaces are moving to a more casual dress code[23], career fairs are the time to make a good first impression in person rather than just sending in a résumé. It is for this reason that you should dress in traditional business attire. The Balance Careers website breaks down this dress code for both men and women, respectively, as follows[24]:

Men	*Women*
❖ Formal suit *or* upscale sports jacket and slacks	❖ Skirt suit *or* pantsuit
	❖ Formal business blouse or top
❖ Tie	❖ Stockings
❖ Business shirt	❖ Closed toe and heel leather shoes
❖ Leather dress shoes	
❖ Appropriate, conservative leather accessories (portfolio or notebook)	❖ Appropriate business accessories (leather portfolio or folder for pad of paper)
❖ Watch (optional)	❖ Subtle jewelry, makeup, and perfume
❖ Subtle cologne	

These lists can be overwhelming (and expensive), but the items create an essential look you should have in your arsenal whenever you may need it. If funding is a concern, go to a secondhand store like Goodwill® and get the necessary components from there. Ultimately, the amount of money you spend on your attire does not matter as long as it is prepared well. This means that your outfit is clean, pressed, and fits you well. Also make a point to wear the outfit before the career fair and become comfortable wearing it. Doing this will help with your confidence when it comes time for the event.

Your college or university should have a listing of the companies attending the career fair on your school's website. Along with those companies will hopefully be a list of what they are looking for in their applicants by major. If not, you can always research the companies themselves and see exactly what they are looking for (as discussed previously). While researching these companies, you should identify those that will help you fulfill your entry-level goal, whether in the form of an internship or a full-time job—and make a point to visit their booth. Know what they are about and prepare yourself with questions to ask them. Refer to the list of sample questions in the "Interviewing" section later in this chapter, but don't limit yourself to just that list.

After your research, you should have a list of about half a dozen companies to talk to about potential opportunities. Your school will hopefully have a map showing where these companies will be located with respect to the event hall. While you should get that map at the door when you check in, you should also review the map online beforehand, if you can, to plan where you need to go to get to the companies you wish to talk to. Prior to the event, print out the map and circle those companies you plan to visit. When you are handed a map at the door, double-check it for any last-minute adjustments that impact your route.

Along with the map, print out two résumés for each company you plan on talking to. If your resources permit it, purchase résumé paper to help stand out among the masses. Résumé paper differs from standard print paper in its color and weight. Résumé paper is manila and heavier, giving it a more professional aesthetic. You've put in so much work on your résumé up to this point; putting it on plain printer paper does not do it justice. If you remember the three-course meal analogy from Chapter 3, think of preparing your printed résumé as the plating of your dish: You want fine dining for your résumé, not Waffle House®.

Career fair recruiter engagements will likely start with a firm handshake and a warm greeting followed by the tried-and-true question, "Tell me a little bit about yourself." The answer to this question should be an elevator pitch—a 30-second summary of why you're a good fit to work for that company. You have only a moment to make a first impression, so it is critical to have a pitch that makes that impression a good one. There are myriad resources online about how to create your pitch; however, yours should be original, captivating, and open-ended so that the recruiter can ask you questions about your experiences. And remember to rehearse it before the career fair! Reading it off a notecard looks unprofessional, and if you stumble on it, you appear unprepared. Practice with your peer network or even a mentor from whom you can get honest feedback on the content; get comfortable reciting it in front of others.

Following the pitch, there will likely be questions from the recruiter and then an opportunity for you to ask questions. Effectively, this is a mini-interview—some companies might even be doing speed interviews—and I will discuss more on handling these in the next section. At the end of the engagement, give the recruiter your résumé, a handshake, and a fond farewell, preferably stating your hopes to hear from them soon, and then move on to your next engagement and repeat the process.

I suggest bringing a small drawstring bag to the career fair. Recruiters tend to offer company swag (branded merchandise) at career fairs, and your hands might get full depending on how many companies you speak to. Having somewhere to put it all will be a nice convenience for you, and the recruiters might even be impressed with your thorough preparation.

Ideally, in the days or weeks following the career fair, the recruiter you spoke to or another member of the Human

Resources staff for the company will reach out to you about applying for a position. From there, apply for the position using the same advice given for online applications. Then send a note to the person who reached out to you to let the individual know that you have applied. If you don't hear back from a recruiter you spoke with at a career fair, apply anyway and then send an email to the recruiter saying how much you enjoyed your conversation and that you applied to whatever role the person recommended.

Aside from career fair engagements, I do not recommend applying in person. You should apply online according to the directions in the requisition. Showing up at a company without an invitation will not be received well by a hiring manager. Follow the company's hiring process as instructed and save the face-to-face for your interviews.

Interviewing

So, a recruiter or hiring manager somewhere decided that your application has passed the preliminary screening, and you've been selected to start the interview process. This is no easy feat, so give yourself a pat on the back! But keep in mind that you don't have the job yet, so you still need to be on top of your game through the potential gauntlet of interviews you may have to endure. Interviewing can be intimidating, but you have to remember throughout this process that the people you are talking to are just like you: people. If you get to the interview stage, then you appeared to be a quality candidate on paper. But now you must show your people skills to those interviewing you.

Interviewing in the modern job market can be broken down into three different categories: Human Resources, technical, and behavioral. The HR interview is likely the first interview you will complete. This will be with a recruiter, hiring manager, or other HR representative to determine whether you are a good fit based almost exclusively on the requisition you applied for. So, preparation for these interview questions should center around those points. The interviewer will also cover logistical topics, including pay, location, and benefits, and will explain the rest of the interview process. If you have questions (and you should) regarding these areas, then the HR interview would be the place to ask them.

Unlike the HR interview, which covers the breadth of the requisition requirements, the technical interview covers your depth in those areas. You should prepare with more technical knowledge in those areas by reviewing your coursework or extracurricular experiences relevant to the tasks outlined in the requisition. Keep in mind during a technical interview that these people likely have other things going on, and they have been asked to do this interview. So, be considerate of their time when speaking with them, and do your best to stick within the time allotted.

Behavioral interviews are something I have seen used recently in different application processes. This type of interview is essentially a Meyers-Briggs® style question-and-answer form that returns a personality assessment based on your responses. Personally, I think it is a little unfair to restrict the scope of someone's personality to a test, especially because these questions can be very confusing and subjective. Nevertheless, they are something you might encounter, so you should be aware of them. My best advice for these is to look up the assessment you are going to take and find practice questions to better understand how the test works; that way, you can most accurately define your personality. Answer honestly; do not sacrifice your integrity and try to be someone you're not.

These three interview categories can come in many different formats. The emphasis on a connected world has made it easy for these interviews to take place from anywhere around the world. This ease of electronic communication is beneficial for you, especially if you want an internship or job in a different geographic region. You should be familiar with all of these different interview styles and formats, because you will likely be evaluated on both your ability to handle the logistics of the interview and the content of the interview itself.

Looking Ahead

The working world is driven by meetings, and an increasingly globalized and interconnected world makes it almost impossible to hold meetings in person all the time. Proficiency with communication tools is essential to ensure that the meetings you are involved with are focused on accomplishing tasks, not on overcoming logistical headaches.

In-Person

Despite the plethora of communication tools in the world, the in-person interview is still a thing. Preparation for these interviews is similar to your preparation for career fairs: Dress business traditional, bring several résumés (on résumé paper, preferably), deliver firm handshakes, and give direct and honest answers to the interviewer's questions. Because of the increased use of remote interviewing, in-person interviews are treated like an event. Therefore, you might speak to several people in one visit; so, plan accordingly. If you have questions prior to the interview, be sure to ask the recruiter or hiring manager you've been working with.

After the day is over, it is best practice to write handwritten thank-you notes to those with whom you met to express your gratitude for their time and attention. Handwritten thank-you notes are a dying art form, and this action will favorably set you apart among your peers and leave a lasting positive impression on the individuals who have a say in hiring you. A good friend of mine with minimal industry experience wrote a thank-you note to the CEO of the company (whom she interviewed with), and he was so impressed with the politeness and professionalism of the gesture that he called her upon receipt of the note and gave her an internship. It's a small act that can make a tremendous impact.

Speed

Speed interviews are one of a few derivations of the in-person interview. You'll most likely experience these at career fairs or professional networking events. Unlike traditional in-person interviews, you have to be quick with your elevator pitch and agile with your responses to questions. Due to their brief and rather impersonal style, a follow-up email is a way to thank the interviewer for his or her time as well as to provide any additional information you find relevant (e.g., digital copy of your résumé, cover letter, more detailed responses to questions).

Group

Another derivation of the in-person interview is group interviews, where you are interviewed at the same time as others interviewing for the same position, or where multiple individuals are interviewing you. If it is you alongside multiple candidates, follow the advice provided for in-person interviews while also maintaining respect for those other candidates. In this format, the interview is in part meant to test how you interact with those around you in a pseudo-professional setting. If you are being interviewed by multiple interviewers, be sure to ask and answer all of their questions in a manner that does not show bias toward one interviewer over another, and also make eye contact with each person as appropriate.

Overnights

In some instances, you might be invited to an overnight event with other candidates vying for different positions within a company. This is not a vacation, nor a chance for you to get a free trip somewhere on some company's dime. It's a job interview, and you should look at the event as if everything you do is being evaluated. Throughout your stay, you should hold yourself to the highest manner of professionalism possible and be respectful of anyone and everyone you interact with from the highest executives to the venue staff (though you should do this always regardless of the environment). Fully participate in all activities and functions, come prepared with questions for your hosts, and network with the other attendees as well as current employees. After the event, send handwritten thank-you notes to those who organized the event, expressing your gratitude for the opportunity to attend.

Phone Call

In my opinion, phone calls are some of the easiest interviews to prepare for because there is no face-to-face interaction. This format allows you to have resources, such as your résumé or interview notes, readily available to review throughout the interview without appearing rude or unprepared as you would if the interview were in-person. Before a phone interview, make sure you are in a quiet space where you will have little distraction and you are comfortable. The more relaxed you are, the more confident you will appear over the phone. If you have one available, complete the interview while looking at yourself in the mirror. I heard this tip somewhere and have done it in my phone interviews ever since. This strategy tricks your brain into thinking you're talking to yourself, which can help boost your confidence and help you interview better. If you find yourself in a multi-connection phone interview, make sure to be respectful of people talking and wait for appropriate queues to speak. This type is by far the most complex interview I've had to do from a logistics perspective, because it's difficult to know when to start talking. Once the interview is done, send an email to the interviewers thanking them for their time. Because phone calls are less personal compared to in-person, an email is sufficient in place of a handwritten note. If you don't have the contact information of the interviewers, ask the person who coordinated the interview to pass on your note of thanks.

Teleconference

The teleconference combines the in-person interview format with the flexibility of a phone call. Unlike the phone, where you have to be cognizant of only your audio, the teleconference requires you to be aware of your surroundings as well. This means that you should dress in business attire from at least the waist up, and your backdrop should be somewhat professional, such as a bookshelf or a plain wall. You can still have notes on your computer; however, you must make sure that you still appear engaged with the interviewer in the event you do choose to look over something. Once it's over, send an email or handwritten note thanking the interviewer for his or her time.

Recorded Response

Recorded response interviews are another innovation of the modern day. Similar to a teleconference in that you are communicating on video, questions appear on your screen, and you record your responses to these questions after a few moments of preparation. Because it is still a video, apply the dress code and environment requirements from the teleconference. These questions will sometimes have limits to the amount of time you have to prepare and respond, as well as to the number of retries you have to answer the question. If you are aware that you are having a recorded response interview, then it is best to prepare for the questions as best as you can ahead of time by reviewing your technical knowledge and extracurricular experience.

Regardless of the category or form they take, all interviews have the same fundamental structure: a greeting, questions from the interviewer, questions from the interviewee, and a farewell. The greeting and farewell are easy and rely on just being a courteous individual (e.g., "Good morning, thank you for having me," "Thanks very much for your time. I look forward to hearing from you soon," or some variation of the two). The challenge then becomes preparing for the questions themselves, both what you will be asked and what you will ask the interviewer.

Interview questions take three different forms: logistical, soft-skill, and hard-skill. Logistical questions are related to the overall nature of the job, including location, pay, work environment, benefits, and so forth. These will likely be the easiest to answer because they generally require a "yes or no" response. Either you want to work at this location or not, the salary works for you or doesn't, and the like. Aside from the consideration of family, you should try to remain as open and flexible to these questions as possible. It's a competitive market, so you really cannot afford to be picky especially if a role can help put your career on the right path early on.

Soft-skill questions relate to your overall person, not necessarily to your field of study. These involve areas like leadership, decision-making, time management, and teamwork. Soft-skill questions are asked to determine how good of a worker you will be, so this is where your extracurricular experience comes into play. You should be safe with having an example of your experience ready for each of the following:

- ❖ A time when you were in charge of a team
- ❖ A time when you had to make a difficult decision
- ❖ A time when you had to resolve a conflict
- ❖ A time when you made something better than when you found it

Include for each of these examples some details of the occasion that really highlight the efforts and accomplishments that were involved. Having solid examples prepared will make your interview run more smoothly and help to paint you in a better light.

Hard-skill questions relate to your coursework, side projects, and relevant work experience. These questions will likely be based on either the requisition, your identification of a time when you fulfilled the role or responsibility given, or the experience listed on your résumé. Preparing for these questions involves going back to the requisition and your experience, and ensuring that you are clear on all points and able to speak with confidence and in greater detail on all of them, both in the requisition and in your résumé.

While the preceding points should cover the basis for the majority of your questions, there is always the curveball question for which you could not have possibly prepared. The best way to handle these off-the-wall questions is to simply say that you don't know and that you will have to follow up with the interviewer on that. This response is very impactful to an interviewer, because it not only shows that you are willing to swallow your pride and admit to not knowing something, but also demonstrates professionalism in how you handle adversity quickly and effectively. A good friend of mine actually received a sales internship with a major healthcare provider in part because he answered an interviewer's question in this way. Also, be sure to document the question and actually follow up on it when you send a thank-you note to the interviewer (i.e., either an email or handwritten note).

Be sure you take advantage of your opportunity to ask questions. Asking questions shows that you are engaged in the interview and that you care about the job and the company enough that you want to learn more about both. My rule of thumb is to prepare at least 3–4 questions before every interview. In my applications for internships and first full-time jobs, the questions tended to look something like this:

❖ (For recruiter or HR interviews) Aside from salary and experience, are there any benefits to this position (e.g., certifications, 401k match)?

❖ What do the opportunities for advancement look like at this company?

❖ How long have you been with the company? Have you enjoyed it?

❖ (For HR interviews) What are the next steps in the process?

❖ (For technical interviews) What does your day-to-day work look like?

❖ (For technical interviews) Do you see any skill gaps that I can work on filling now so that I can be better prepared in the event that I become a part of the team?

Listen to and digest their answers because they can be useful in determining whether the role is a good fit for you as well as give you the chance to ask follow-up questions based on the responses. As part of your thank-you follow-up, be sure to express your gratitude for their answers to your questions and to mention how those were helpful in determining that the role is a good fit.

Interviewing can be challenging, but it is especially difficult if you do not prepare. The more preparation you put in prior to the interview itself, the more confident you will be when you do the real thing. At the end of the day, an interview should just feel like a natural conversation between two (or more) adults, because that's all it is. If you're professional, polite, and prepared, then you should be just fine.

Ask the Experts

Brian Herndon, Lead Technical Recruiting Manager at AT&T

Brian was my recruiter throughout the hiring process of my first job. He reached out to me on LinkedIn about a potential opportunity, we set up a call, and 3 months later I accepted the job offer. Throughout the process, Brian was transparent, friendly, and displayed a great deal of professionalism. Without a doubt, he was one of—if not—the best recruiter I worked with throughout my college career, and I trust that his insights will help you as you begin your journey in the hiring process.

Tell me about yourself, your career, and your current role.

As a 2006 graduate of Georgia Southern University with a degree in Sport Management, I initially worked for a professional hockey team, the Florida Panthers, in South Florida as a part of the sales organization. After two seasons, I made the switch to AT&T through our B2B (business to business) sales program. I came to AT&T for the training, earning potential, and stability after witnessing a very volatile sports industry. After joining AT&T in 2009, I was in Atlanta for 6 months of sales training before moving to Birmingham for 2½ years in a small business sales role. From there I moved to Dallas as a part of AT&T's College Recruiting team, focusing on recruiting for the same sales program that I went through. After 3 years in that role, I moved into Business Marketing, where I served as part of the Chief of Staff team supporting the Chief Marketing Officer. After about 18 months, I moved back into college recruiting where I have supported our Technology Development Program, Cybersecurity Development Program, Entertainment Group, and Chief Data Office.

As a recruiter, what do you look for in candidates for the positions you're filling? In general, how are candidates evaluated?

For all roles, we focus on skills, experience, and education. For technical hires, technical skills are table stakes. You *have* to have software skills for a software engineering role.

We love to see those who have been able to apply what has been learned in the classroom, which is why internships and work experience are so important. Communication skills are incredibly important as well—not just presentation skills, but the ability to effectively cross-functionally communicate. Can you take technical information and explain it to someone from our product marketing group? Finding strong communication skills among technical talent is extremely important to the success of our program.

What are some of the most common mistakes you see in interviews and how would you suggest they be fixed?

- ❖ Lack of preparation. You can bank on certain questions being asked in a behavioral interview, so be ready with examples of overcoming obstacles, working in teams, failures, persistence, and the like. Any Google search will give you a list of questions to prepare for.
- ❖ Don't ramble. Listen to the question and answer it. You can definitely provide additional context and supporting information to make your answer more credible, but stay on topic.

❖ Appearance. You don't need to be in a suit for a video interview, but you don't need to be in a hoodie either. If you aren't going to take the interview seriously, will you take the job seriously?

❖ Questions. Do you have good questions at the end of the interview? Ask questions about the company (e.g., direction of the business, culture, benefits), the position (i.e., clarifying questions about the nature of the work), and the next steps (e.g., Am I a good fit? Do you expect me to be included in the next round of interviews? What is the timeline?).

In contrast, what makes for a successful interviewee? What traits do see in high performers?

❖ Conversation skills. I don't need to be friends with you, but we need to be able to easily maintain a professional conversation. As an interviewer, I can understand nerves in the beginning, but can you get past that and put together complete answers?

❖ Technical communication. I do not come from a computer science background. Early in the interview, you will know that about me. Can you take complex projects and explain them in a way that is understood by anyone, regardless of the person's field of study?

❖ Want the job you are interviewing for. Great interviews are with candidates who want to work for the company and in the job for which they applied. I can't tell you how many times I interviewed someone for a sales role that admitted he or she preferred product marketing. I would encourage you to apply only for jobs you want! We can tell during the interview if you aren't passionate about the position.

❖ Wear pants. I had an interview via webcam with a candidate who spilled coffee on himself during the interview. Naturally, his first reaction was to stand up. He looked great from the waist up. We'll just say he was less formal from the waist down.

Where do you see the most failure in candidates during the hiring process? What can they do to mitigate these faults?

Résumé screen. We likely screen out 50% of applicants prior to the first interview. Your résumé *must* reflect the best version of yourself. Ensure that it is laid out in a logical fashion and highlights the best of your experience. Here are a couple of points:

❖ Use quantifiable data where possible.

❖ Use bullets, not paragraphs.

❖ Grammar is important.

❖ For STEM (science, technology, engineering, and mathematics) folks, call out your specific proficiencies.

❖ Don't include an objective unless you tailor it to every position you apply for. A general objective on your résumé is too vague and doesn't express interest in a specific position or company.

❖ Keep to one page if possible.

From waiting in line to the final goodbye, what makes for the perfect career fair engagement as a recruiter?

Confident, articulate, concise. Career fairs are crazy for candidates, but they are crazy for employers too. Maintain a good handshake and look the recruiter in the eye. Once you determine what we are recruiting for, do your best to highlight some of the experience you have gained that is relevant to the role. Also, quickly highlight leadership positions.

You want to leave the conversation with a clear direction for next steps. Ask for the recruiter's card or email address. Indicate your interest in the position and that you will apply after the event. Then apply and follow up! Do your best to find something to differentiate yourself from other candidates that you can refer to in your follow-up email. If during the career fair you find that you are both Atlanta Hawks fans, reference that in your follow-up email. This will help the recruiter remember who you are on a day when the recruiter met 300 students. Tip: If you get a business card, immediately after you leave the conversation, jot down a few notes on the card of what you talked about to help your follow-up seem more credible.

What information are you looking for while you listen to an elevator pitch?

A number of things. Communication skills are key, but so is the substance. Can you effectively articulate your experience so that someone from any background (tech or non-tech) can understand? Quickly be able to highlight your most meaningful project and some of the technical skills you used to be successful. Give me 30–45 seconds of why you might stand apart from the 300 students I meet during a career fair.

Is there any other advice you would give to those entering the hiring process?

❖ Pursue your interests! Recruiters want to hire people who are excited about the company and role.

❖ Do your research—on everything. This includes the company, the recruiter through LinkedIn, industry, and so forth.

❖ Be aggressive. Proactively engage on LinkedIn with messaging to the recruiter informing that person of your application.

❖ Be available. When I ask for interview availability, some provide a 30-minute window a week from the request. I understand that every schedule is different, but being flexible for the interviewer is helpful.

Wrap-Up

Up to this chapter, you have been in direct control of everything you did in your college career, including your academic affairs, extracurricular activities, and ways in which you convey those experiences. Unfortunately, you are not in control of the job you get. You can't just go to the job store, pick yourself out a fancy new job, and ring it up at the register. You have to find the job or internship that is best for you, apply, and interview in the hopes that you beat out the other applicants to get that role.

In 2008, I remember sitting with my family watching Michael Phelps attempt to earn eight gold medals in a single Olympics—an unprecedented feat. When it came to the 100m Butterfly, his best race, he came within one one-hundredth of a second of losing that race. It was later revealed that halfway through the race his goggles flooded, and the only way he could discern how far he was to the end of the lap was based on counting the number of strokes he was taking. Meanwhile, the swimmer ahead of Phelps appeared that he was going to beat the Olympic favorite. In the final second, however, Phelps's opponent seemed to turn his head slightly as to see where Phelps was with respect to himself. That slight turn of the head slowed him down enough for Phelps, temporarily blinded, to pass the swimmer and go on to achieve those eight gold medals. Had Phelps's opponent focused on himself, he would have won.

The same analogy applies to you in the hiring process. In this case, you are Michael Phelps, and the other hundreds if not thousands of applicants are your opponents. You have all the tools necessary to succeed, and you know the number of strokes it takes to get to the end of the pool. But if you lose sight of your goals, then you might just end up coming in second. Keep your head down, put in the hard work, and hopefully you'll come out with your gold medal: the job offer you've worked so hard for.

Chapter 5

Internships and Co-Ops: Welcome to the Real World

Internships and cooperative education programs (co-ops) are opportunities for you to gain the real-world experience employers are looking for, so that you can enter a full-time role when you graduate and dive right into work. In fact, internship participation among college students has been steadily increasing over the last 25 years and has apparently been the threshold for determining who will make up the entry-level workforce[25]. This increase is because internships and co-ops reduce the risk for employers who want to see how you work in a professional setting as well as how you fit with the company.

It's like a job with a 90-day warranty: If they don't like you, then they can just send you back (a little crass, but it gets the point across). If they do like you, then they can (and will do their best to) keep you.

However, just getting an internship alone will not land you the job you want upon graduation. In fact, poor performance in an internship can alienate you from employment with that company. In contrast, excellent performance in an internship (and then effectively marketing your skills afterward) can lead to a plethora of other opportunities both with that company and beyond—perhaps including the job of your dreams. In this chapter, I talk about how to be a high performer in your internship or co-op so that the company is more than eager to bring you back full time once you graduate.

Pre-orientation

Before you even step foot in the office, you should be preparing for your new role. If you have to relocate for the role, be sure to have all the logistics of your move settled before your start date. Having those logistics out of the way will free up your time to focus on your work from the very start. If you have any issues with your relocation, work with your new company's Human Resources representative and make that person aware of any potential problems, especially if they impact your start date.

Speaking of Human Resources, you will likely get a pre-orientation email with all the information you need before you start working with your new company. This information should include basic expectations, such as how to get into the building on your first day, what IDs and other information to bring on your first day, and when you should arrive for day one and orientation. Carefully review this email and fulfill the requests asked by the HR department. Again, you want to do everything in your power not to be the bad cog in the machine; you need to make a good impression on your first day of work. If you have any questions before your start date or if you do not see an email like this, then be sure to send an email to the HR department and ask for the information you need to start on the right foot.

Two things that you will likely need to complete prior to onboarding for any position are the I-9 form and a drug test. The I-9 is an employment verification service used by the United States to verify identity and ability to work. You will need to bring identification items or documents from a specified list to support the I-9 form; however, a U.S. passport is sufficient for verifying both your identity and your ability to work. Have the required documents ready and with you on your first day of work. For more information about the I-9, visit www.uscis.gov/i-9.

As for the drug test, the timeline is more variable than the I-9. I have worked for companies that drug tested within 48 hours of accepting the offer and companies that did not drug test at all. The bottom line is that if you are preparing for internships and job offers, you really shouldn't be using any kind of illegal substance. No high is worth sacrificing your career, let alone a great job or internship. Your employer will reach out to you with instructions for your test. Follow those instructions to the letter; otherwise you might lose your job before it even begins.

In the days leading up to your first day, you should prepare to make a good first impression once again. While your office dress code might be smart casual on a daily basis, you're the new kid in town, and you should dress to impress for your first day. Find that outfit you wore to a career fair or your in-person interview (or get one, if you didn't earlier) and take it to the cleaners. After the first day, you can start dialing back based on what the other folks in the office wear day-to-day. It's always better to be overdressed than underdressed at first. However, if your office is super casual and employees wear polos and jeans every day, don't be that person who wears a suit and tie every day to stand out. Frankly, you'll just look silly. Use your best judgment on what works and follow the trend accordingly.

Aside from your well-groomed and professionally dressed self, you should also plan to bring three items: a notepad, a pen, and a folder. You are guaranteed to receive a mountain of information on your first day, both orally and on paper. You need to be prepared to document key points as needed as well as keep your notes in a place where you can refer to them later. While your company might provide these supplies for you, it is always better not to leave anything to chance. So, make the investment; go to an office supply store and bring your own. As the old Boy Scout saying goes, "Be prepared."

Orientation Day

On your first day, take a deep breath and revel in the fact that you've reached a huge milestone. You're about to start meaningful work and get real exposure to your industry. You'll probably have that excited-nervous feeling in your gut (I remember I did), but keep in mind that you've been preparing for months, if not years, leading up to this day. You've earned a seat at the table, and I congratulate you on your achievement.

Orientation day can vary in length from a half-day to a full week. It all depends on your company. As I mentioned in the "Pre-orientation" section, be ready to receive a lot of information. This information will be primarily HR-related at first to help you assimilate with the company at-large, and then move into onboarding with your team and your role from there. Honestly, this orientation can be a very boring process, but it will be invaluable for you to get a good start. There are usually breaks built into the program and other fun icebreaker activities as well to alleviate some of the mundaneness. You'll likely be onboarding with other interns, so be sure to introduce yourself and be polite to your fellow onboardees as well as to the staff running the orientation.

Plan to show up at least 15 minutes ahead of time on your first day (remember about being present, covered in Chapter 1). Getting an early start will ensure you have plenty of time to find the office and parking as well as start networking with your fellow coworkers before orientation. Throughout your orientation, be attentive and take notes as needed. Be a sponge and absorb all this information. If your fellow interns have questions later, they can look to you later as a keeper of all this info. You will receive a lot of logistical information about your role that will be important for you to know during your employment. If you have questions, do not be afraid to ask them. While I don't believe in "no such thing as a stupid question," I do believe that it is better to ask a stupid question to avoid a mistake than to make a stupid mistake that could have been avoided by asking a question.

I briefly mentioned icebreakers. These are activities to get you talking with the other on boardees and excited about working at the company. Some of the activities I've done include a mock PR campaign for a social outreach program, a word bubble about what experiences we want to get out of the internship, and that tower challenge where you have to build the tallest tower with marshmallows and raw spaghetti. At face value, they seem really silly and don't add a whole lot of value to your experience. However, they're a really good way to interact with your peers and see how the team dynamics play out (like when you formed your peer network). As silly as they may be, you should actively participate in the icebreakers if you have them. It makes you look as if you aren't a team player if you do not, and it also might come off as rude to the event planner.

Speaking of the event planner, keep that person in mind as you go through orientation. Planning these events and preparing to onboard a new group of employees or interns is no easy feat. If you find something you think could be improved, give some constructive feedback after the orientation, if prompted. Regardless, be sure to thank the coordinator for his or her time in planning and holding the event.

Your primary objective during your internship or co-op is to learn as much as you can in the amount of time you work at the company. Orientation is the start of this learning experience and likely your first taste of the working world. Keep an open mind throughout the process and make the most of it beyond your first days of orientation. Later on, orientation may be a fun topic to joke about with your new coworkers. It's like workplace puberty: Everyone goes through it and it's not the best time, but you'll look back on it and smile.

Day-to-Day

After orientation, you'll start to get into your regular work-flow. Some of the best advice I received as I started my first internship—aside from what I gleaned from the popular movie *Office Space*—was that you are not expected to know anything as an intern. While you should have some skills from coursework and extracurriculars, ultimately internships and co-ops give you the means to get real work experience you otherwise couldn't get. This means that the standard for your success is frankly very low. Couple this with the negative stigma associated with millennial workers[26], and you have an incredible opportunity to demonstrate high performance and ultimately get a full-time job. It all boils down to a few basics.

Do your job

You were hired based on your ability to accomplish the roles and responsibilities of the job. Intern work is not the most difficult and can even be pretty dull at times. Still, you have a job to do. Remember that unlike school, which give you a grade based on how well you complete a task, the real world operates on a pass-fail basis. You do the job, or you don't. If you do the work and do it well, you get commended. If you don't, then you might find yourself without an offer at the end of your employment term.

Another thing to remember is that internships and co-ops are temporary employment, and while they might turn into a full-time role, there is no guarantee. The work you do is meaningful in some way to the company, and so you want to ensure that it can continue to be of value to the organization if you don't return. That is why I highly recommend thoroughly documenting everything you do and labeling that documentation clearly. This documentation will ensure that people can build on your work when you leave and will make the impact of your work more lasting.

Looking Ahead

Things happen in life that are unexpected. If someone leaves a company abruptly or passes away, that resource of knowledge is lost to the organization and hinders business continuity. Documenting your work and disseminating it helps to prevent that from happening, allowing business to continue smoothly when the unexpected in life happens.

Do more than your job

As stated earlier, internships are a chance to learn more about the company, your industry, and the working world as a whole. With this in mind, you should explore other opportunities to broaden your horizons, meet other people, and learn different skill sets. In one of my internships, my primary role was a security analyst. Halfway through that summer, I ended up working on a special project developing a monitoring tool for a different team. Not only did I learn so much more than I had anticipated, but I also gained skill sets that helped me get my first full-time job.

If you are interested in working on a special project, ask your manager whether it would be okay to work on something extra. You might be part of a team that needs your full attention on the work you are tasked for, and your manager will be able to evaluate this for you. Your primary role should always be your number one priority; however, if you find that you have some slack time, or if you find that you could better help your team elsewhere, then it might be worth pursuing that opportunity either as part of your role or in place of it. If you are approved to work on a special project, consult the team or your intern program lead to see whether there is anything you can work on. And if you at any point need help, don't be afraid to ask for it.

Ask questions

As an intern, you are not expected to know much, if anything, about what you are supposed to be doing. If you act like you know everything, you're likely going to be regarded unfavorably by your peers and coworkers. Much like the kid who wore glasses in *The Polar Express*, nobody likes a know-it-all. Be present and try to learn as much as you can.

Asking questions is so important for getting the most out of your internship. Soliciting information, rather than assuming you know it already, will improve your performance. You'll have a better understanding of what the expectations are, and you will be more respected by those around you. Most people I've met, as well as myself, enjoy answering questions about their work, career, and personal life. Humans are inherently social beings, but technology has made us more introverted. Taking the first step to ask questions demonstrates leadership and will help you with the next topic.

Network

Internships and co-ops allow you to see into the working world and to meet both professionals and fellow students in your industry. During your employment, you'll likely work on projects, go on outings, and make small talk with these people on a regular basis. After working with them for some time, don't be afraid to reach out to them and add them to your network. If you've been following the advice in this book, they'll likely be eager to have you as part of their network because of your work ethic and professionalism. After connecting with them, be sure to follow up on a somewhat regular basis. There is a reason LinkedIn tells you when a person in your network has a work anniversary or birthday. It's an opportunity to reconnect, and people like to be recognized on those events.

Outside of your normal work, internships and co-ops can offer other opportunities for executive level networking in the form of a "lunch and learn." Some of these sessions might be in-person while others might be remote. In either instance, these events are very worthwhile, and you should actively participate in them. Not many people receive the level of executive exposure you get from networking sessions like these, and the information given by these presenters is often relevant to your career growth. These people have worked their entire adult lives to grow into their current roles, and at one point they were where you are now. Listen and learn from them and ask questions if you have the opportunity. When the session is over, send a follow-up email or note to thank them for their time.

If you're feeling really ambitious, you can ask one of these individuals to lunch. This is a great opportunity to get one-on-

one time with executives to better understand their career paths and ask for their advice about your own career. During my second internship following a "lunch and learn" with the CTO (Chief Technology Officer) of the company I was working for, I sent her a thank-you email for answering a question I had. She replied and mentioned that she was coming to our office in the coming weeks, and we ended up going to lunch. This was a great opportunity to learn what she does in her role, how she got there through her career, and what she would do if she were my age now to be better prepared for her role.

All these basic tasks come down to one thing: learning. You have been granted an incredible opportunity with whatever company or organization you are working for to learn as much as you can in preparation for your future career. Leverage the experiences and knowledge you gain in these few short months in your communication pieces (your résumé and LinkedIn, primarily), keep up with those you meet in your network, and don't forget to have fun through it all.

Last Week and Beyond

As your internship comes to a close, you'll likely have an off-boarding interview. This will probably be with your manager or a member of the HR staff to talk about your role, the internship program, and your future. This is when your performance over the last several weeks is highlighted, along with the rest of the work you have done thus far in your undergrad career.

The most important thing you can do in these interviews is be perfectly honest while remaining polite. If you loved your job, tell the person. If you hated your position, but loved the company, phrase it like, "I could really see myself somewhere within the organization" or something to that effect. If you're a high performer, the company is going to want to keep you. If that means shifting roles in your next internship or full-time position, then be open to having those conversations. However, at no point should you say that you don't want to return to the company. Even if you don't intend to return, saying that closes the opportunity to work for that company in the event that you don't have another option.

Depending on your role, it might be worthwhile to request to continue your work in a part-time capacity while you're still in school. This is a dream scenario, because you can continue to get work experience (and possibly paid) while also completing your degree. If you have the chance to continue, you'll have to be diligent about managing your time. But the preparedness you gain will make it all worth it because you will graduate with more real-world work experience. Though working part-time could happen, do not assume this will occur. Your manager must approve your continued hours and clear them with the necessary channels.

If you do end up continuing to work while you're in school, realize that this is a privilege, and you should make every effort to maintain your high performance both academically and in your work. Having a job might mean that some of your extracurriculars will be put on the back burner; but if your goal is to get a career out of college, then you'll have to prioritize as needed. You don't have that first job yet, and your work is not done until you walk across that stage and move into your full-time role.

As part of your internship, you might have to deliver a final presentation summarizing the work you did during the summer.

My advice for these presentations is to prepare early and practice often. Make sure your presentation flows logically and adequately reflects the work you've done over the course of your tenure. As you practice, ask the fellow interns you've met and worked with all summer to practice with you and bounce ideas off one another. This practice is a great way to get honest feedback before you deliver your presentation to management. And if you are afraid of public speaking, aside from practice, I recommend thinking of your audience as one person. If you imagine you are having a conversation with a friend, you will feel more relaxed during your presentation.

As you prepare to leave your role and return to school, be sure other members of your team are aware of the work you've done. To ensure a smooth transition, schedule meetings with them before you leave to go over your work and how it relates to the day-to-day operations of your group. Ask the team members what questions they have about what you worked on and do your best to answer them. Show your teammates the documentation you've created and ask them to review it in case anything is unclear. It's one thing to write documentation, but it's another thing to write documentation that is discernible by others.

While your last day might mean your last time at the company, it doesn't mean your last time working with the people you've been with over the past several months. The connections you've made during your internship or co-op will carry on through the rest of your career and will be invaluable to both you and them. That's why you should be sure to thank those who have helped you during your tenure and make a point to stay in touch with them as you begin your career and throughout it. For those that were especially impactful (e.g., your manager, a mentor), I'd recommend writing them a handwritten thank-you note and getting them a small gift. They will appreciate the sentiment, and it will show them how much you appreciated the help they gave you. Beyond your coworkers, stay in touch with your fellow interns. They understand what you're going through as you continue your coursework and might even be able to give you leads for other opportunities down the road.

Speaking of continuing your coursework, returning to school after working might feel like a drag. Your newly found income and the relief from the rigors of coursework might deter you from returning and instead drive you to go right to work. I'll remind you of the whole point of this book: two pieces of paper. To get the job you want—and probably a job with that very company you just worked for—you need to have a college degree. My first employer actually solicited verification that I had gotten the degree I said I did; if I didn't pass, then I would have lost my position. Even if you do not have to undergo an education check, you will likely still hit a glass ceiling when it comes to jobs, or at the very least, you will lose a position to someone with better credentials. Stick it out and finish your degree; the working world will be waiting for you when you get back to it.

As you return to school, take full advantage of the knowledge you learned in your internships and co-ops. I found myself pulling a great deal of the knowledge I learned in my work experiences and applying it to my coursework. If you do it right, school should be exponentially easier after your first internship and will hopefully light a fire under you to finish so you can get back to work. As you find yourself using your experiences, be sure to disseminate this knowledge to your educational peers. College is about learning from one another as much as it is learning from a professor, and we all come from various backgrounds. Bringing your experiences to the table and learning from those of others will make everyone more qualified in the end.

Ask the Experts

Jim Kelly, President and CEO of Invictus International Consulting, LLC

Mr. Kelly has had an incredible career of both military and professional service. Objectively speaking, he is one of the most successful people I have had the pleasure of meeting in my life, and he is equally as kind and personable. Through his career, he has determined how to be successful in business, as well as what traits in people further drive that success and what traits hinder it. I trust that his words will help you as you perform not only in your internships, but also in your professional career and personal life.

Can you tell me a little bit about yourself, your service background, your career path, and what you do in your current role as CEO of a company?

I am a former Naval Intelligence Officer with more than 30 years of leadership experience within the National, Strategic, Intelligence, and Defense communities.

As CEO/President/Managing Member of Invictus International Consulting, my third company, I oversee the day-to-day operations of the firm, which focuses on National Security, Defense, and Intelligence services; Information Technology; and consulting services for the U.S. Government and private enterprises. The company recently won a significant Information Security Contract at the Defense Intelligence Agency (DIA).

As Vice President and General Manager (VP/GM) for Computer Sciences Corporation's (CSC's) Army Division and the lead executive for CSC's business with the DIA and the National Geospatial-Intelligence Agency (NGA), I oversaw nearly $1 billion in annual business with employees across the United States, Europe, and the Middle East, and support for combat forces in Afghanistan.

Major business areas I supported included cloud computing solutions, cyber security, enterprise information technology services, military intelligence support, biometrics, training, and C4ISR (Command, Control, Communications, Computer, Intelligence, Surveillance, and Reconnaissance) support. Major programs I helped CSC grow during my tenure include the Army's Logistics Modernization Program (LMP); Army Data Center Consolidation Plan (ADCCP); Program Executive Office for Enterprise Information Systems (PEO-EIS); C4ISR support to Communications and Electronics Command (CECOM); DIA's ORION program; the Army's Distributed Common Ground System (DCGS) and Counter IED (improvised explosive device) Targeting programs; Research, Development, Test, & Evaluation (RDT&E) services for major Army Aviation and Missile Programs; cyber security support to the 24th Air Force and Joint Information Operations Warfare Command (JIOWC) in San Antonio, TX; and the Stone Ghost International Systems program.

Prior to Invictus and CSC, I was the Founder and Managing Partner of two successful small businesses: Centauri Solutions LLC and Hawkeye Systems LLC. Both companies provided program management, information systems and technology, systems engineering, subject matter expertise, and other capabilities to key components of the Intelligence, National Security, and Homeland Security communities. Centauri was a small business started in March 2006, which was acquired by CSC in December 2010. Hawkeye Systems was founded in January 2002. I later became the Chief Operating Officer of Gray Hawk Systems, Inc., Hawkeye's parent company. Both Hawkeye and Gray Hawk were acquired by ManTech® for more than $100 million, where I operated as President/COO of ManTech-Gray Hawk prior to leaving to start Centauri Solutions.

Before Centauri, when I retired from the Navy, I was a Director of Intelligence, representing Syntek Technologies and, along with Admiral John Poindexter (U.S. Naval Academy '58), was one of the two Systems Engineering and Technical Assistance (SETA) leads on the Defense Advanced Research Projects Agency's (DARPA) Project GENOA. The project subsequently became a cornerstone for technology insertion in the campaign against terrorism.

As a Naval Officer, my duties included Surface Warfare Officer during the Iranian Hostage Crisis and the Korean Contingency Operations, Intelligence Officer during Desert Storm and the Iran-Iraq Tanker War, Liaison Officer at National Defence Headquarters (NDHQ) Ottawa, Special Projects Branch Chief for the Director of DIA, Chief of the Global Command & Control System (GCCS) Branch for the Joint Chiefs of Staff (JCS-J2), Director of the Information and Research Division of the United Nations' Situation Centre, and Chief of Staff for the Joint Deployable Intelligence Support Systems (JDISS) Program Office.

I hold a Bachelor of Science degree in Naval Engineering from the U.S. Naval Academy, as well as a Master of Science in Operations Research and Systems Analysis from the Naval Postgraduate School in Monterey, CA.

What from your service in the United States Navy has made a lasting impression in your professional career?

- ❖ Being responsible
- ❖ Working hard
- ❖ Never taking anything for granted
- ❖ Having to learn to hit the curve ball
- ❖ Never failing your troops
- ❖ "Say it–Do it," stop talking start doing
- ❖ Serving the country and your fellow man, which gives one tremendous satisfaction
- ❖ Having to earn respect . . . it is not given

What inspired you to start not one or two, but three companies? What drives you to not only succeed, but also to continue to succeed?

I never really thought about starting my own company, but after 9/11, I felt like I needed to do more for the country and I had a vision for how to do that. Out of that vision emerged Hawkeye Systems, and the rest is history.

From each company I learned more about people, tactics, and procedures necessary to be successful. Above all, I learned that relationships are the key to success. Making people trust you and believe in you is important. Beyond that, not only what you can bring to the table, but what you stand for, helps build this trust.

I have an internal engine that just will not quit. I have always been driven to lead from as early as 7 or 8 years old when I would organize the neighborhood kids to go to the park or play in the street. This continued in high school and college, where I was Captain of most of the teams I was on.

My drive is internal; I am *never* satisfied with status quo, the latest win, or where the company is. I am always driving for the next win or for the company to be more successful so we can touch as many people with our passionate outlook as possible. If we can help defend the country's gates of freedom and help make people's lives better, then we cannot sit idly by. Rather, we must constantly strive for more as well as constantly evolve and improve.

With starting three different companies, I imagine you've had to make a fair amount of difficult decisions in your career. How do you make these decisions with confidence and deal with the consequences when perhaps you did not make the right one?

When you have a company built upon the sweat and tears of great people, difficult decisions are infrequent. When they do arise, your council of talent will give you sound advice and options. With the information at hand, decision-making has to be decisive. Once a decision is made, you stand by it; and if you are wrong, then admit it, remember it, and move on together (always together).

A company wins together and loses together, but to have the right culture where people freely communicate information without fear of repercussions is critical, and a leader must be able to inspire those around him or her in order to create that kind of environment: an environment where Spartans will do anything for you to ensure mission success.

As a leader of people, what traits do you value in the people who work for you?

- ❖ **Passion** People need a passionate commitment to excellence. One of my favorite quotes is, "Live with passion, give your gift!" Be passionate about whatever you do in life, and your gift is you. No one has your education, your community of friends, your family influences, your ups and downs. If you give yourself, that in unto itself is the gift.

- ❖ **Loyalty** Never speak badly about your boss, your company, or your peers. They are your family; and if you don't like the family, then leave. Once gone, you can complain about the company; but while you are being paid by the company, be *most* loyal everywhere, in public in particular. I hold loyalty most dear.

- ❖ **Be Responsible** Take charge of your own life—no excuses. Make your bed, show up on time, represent your company admirably, and look good. No one wants to be your mother or father at work.

- ❖ **Professional** You are a reflection of your company. Always look and act in a professional way. Commit to what you do. How you interact with people as well as how you perform your job will speak volumes. Don't blame others. Do your job. Make it happen.

In contrast, what traits do you perhaps see in people, young people in particular, that hinder their ability to succeed? What advice would you give them to correct those potentially harmful habits?

The younger people typically want it now. They don't necessarily want to spend years working for the objective. Generally speaking, they have had things given to them and haven't had to earn it. Most did not have to work growing up to get money for school or college. Most of those with athletic backgrounds have had trainers who have assisted their development, and they did not have to "do it on their own." Younger people do not understand or stop to think about how others have methodically climbed the ladder. They just want to take the elevator to the top.

They also often lack the interpersonal skills that are the building blocks of successful companies. They prefer social media, emails, texts, and the like to communicate instead of over the phone or—the best method—face-to-face interaction. In general, I believe corporate young people are intimidated to interact with clients (or even office hierarchy) face-to-face. They would rather fall back to the impersonal, electronic interaction.

They also never want to be wrong, so they hesitate instead of aggressively performing certain tasks. I do see the earnestness in young people trying to do the right thing, and that is a good trait. But I also see that some of the young people think they are smarter than their bosses and do not have the intestinal fortitude to hang in there and adjust. This lack of understanding and inflexibility will hinder their success.

Advice? For starters, be humble. You can learn from everyone, no matter what their age. Be as flexible as possible (what I call Max Flex). Live by the four agreements: Be impeccable with your word; *never* take anything personally; don't assume anything; and just do your best! I see unbelievable potential in young business talent; the tidal wave of this youth movement will crush the competition and take this world by storm. These young people just need to stop and smell the roses sometimes, and they will learn the things that will help them maximize their talent and not only be successful, but most of all, be happy!

The name Invictus is inspired by your father and his narration of the poem by that name throughout your childhood. Family is clearly a very important aspect of your life. How have you ensured that you maintain good relationships with your family throughout the commitments required to run a successful company?

Family has always been first in my life, and I hold them close to my heart. To be truly successful in business and in life, you need a balance. While I have dedicated most of my life serving this great country of ours in the military and as a contractor, I have always been there for my wife and sons and their families. At the end of days, it is family—not money, accolades, or prestige—that will be your legacy.

Invictus is the culmination of 40 years of service and by far the best of the three companies. This one is truly built around my vision of God, country, and family by bringing in talented people and working hard toward common goals. We have been able to do some extraordinary things in a very short period of time. We have also established a life balance where we work hard, have fun, and have created an atmosphere of friendship, devotion to duty, and happiness. The company has also given me the gift of being able to work with, coach, and mentor my two sons.

Dad would say that nothing in this world is insurmountable, nothing is beyond our capability, and that even under extreme adversity anything is possible if you believe in yourself and your unconquerable soul. This created a belief in me, as well as many others who have been inspired by the poem, that we can accomplish anything if we work hard enough and never doubt. Dad lived by the trinity of God, America, and family all his life. He touched many lives and, although he never was rich, he was rich in everything that counted—a wonderful wife, the love of his family, and vast friendships across all walks of life.

I try to emulate this philosophy, and I feel it is lacking in America. The poem and the core values set in me by Mom and Dad are what have guided me throughout my life. My war cry of "live with passion, give your gift" is something that I try to instill in all around me. Be passionate about what you do in life, and your gift is yourself.

Is there any other advice you would give young people starting their professional careers?

- ❖ Follow the four agreements.
- ❖ Learn to hit the curve ball.
- ❖ Learn the poem "Invictus" and be the master of your fate.
- ❖ Be quiet and learn, but don't be afraid to speak when you feel you have the right answers or a better way to do things.

Wrap-Up

The movie *Office Space* takes a comical look at corporate life in all its glory (and you should watch it before you start working). For the traditional college student, an internship or co-op is likely your first taste of this realm. Much like college is incredibly different from high school, the working world is much different than college. No more homework (if you do it right), no more lectures, no more exams, and of course (likely) being paid to do something that you are actually passionate about! It's a great opportunity, and you should be excited about it. But remember to keep up the effort until you leave your school with both pieces of paper. Just don't attach them together with your red stapler (a reference you will understand after you watch *Office Space*).

Conclusion

When I turned 21 years old, I started playing a little bit of Blackjack. As I was playing, I realized there was a lot more to the game than just getting to 21 or beating the dealer (notwithstanding the general ambiance of the casino itself). Each hand is different, and each table is stacked differently. Some casinos use automatic shufflers, while some shuffle manually. Sometimes you sit at the head of the table and control the game, while other times you're a victim to an inexperienced player who messes up the rest of the game. But even through the ups and downs on the table or the variables surrounding you, there is one thing that always remains consistent: You have to play the hand you're dealt.

This is a truism I've applied to my everyday life. We're all dealt a different hand in life. Some of us get Blackjack, some of us get a hard 16 (that's a really bad hand, for all of you non-gamblers). Some of us get derailed by other players; and sometimes we have a really good hand, but then the dealer gets 21 and everyone loses. You might be the heir to an empire or a struggling first-generation college student. You might have a rough home life or perhaps you got screwed over by someone who you thought would do you right. In any instance, life inevitably goes on, and you're stuck playing the hand you're dealt.

For a lot of you, this might just mean that you don't know how to play the game (starting a career, I mean). Nobody has ever taught you the rules because you are expected to learn them on your own or from somebody else. Sure, you can Google it; but you can't search for something if you don't know what you're looking for. That's the point of this book: to teach you how to play the game, and hopefully help you to turn your hard 16 into a winning hand. Is it a foolproof system guaranteed to work every time? Probably not. But nothing is ever certain in life; the dealer could always have 21.

Much like you probably believe you know the basics of Blackjack, you probably believed that getting a college degree is enough to get you a job and start a career. Your academic and extracurricular endeavors, along with how you effectively communicate your experience, sell yourself in the hiring process, and performance in internships ultimately embodies what you'll be doing if you want to get a job out of college, not your degree alone. As I said in the very beginning, taking the initiative to read this book shows that you have the motivation to create the success you want for yourself. The coveted prize at the end of the college experience is your two pieces of paper—your Ace and King, a college degree and a job offer.

If you have any questions or want any further help, feel free to reach out to me on LinkedIn, and I will do my very best to help you in any way that I can. Also feel free to let me know about your success, what helped you, or what I can improve in this book. Ultimately, for as much as I want you to succeed, I want to continue to grow as well and help as many people as I can to achieve their dreams of starting a life for themselves. Together, we can all help one another get our two pieces of paper.

About the Author

Skyler W. King is a cyber security product manager originally from Millersville, MD. After graduating from Archbishop Spalding High School in 2014, Skyler went to Louisiana Tech University in pursuit of a degree in Cyber Engineering. There, in keeping with the focus of this book, he thrived, holding three summer internships with three different companies, as well as an in-school position maintaining a student lab facility valued at approximately $500,000. In these positions, Skyler gained vast amounts of industry experience while also learning how best to conquer the realm of starting a career. Upon graduating in 2018, Skyler was hired by a major telecommunications company where he works in 3-1 year rotations in different cyber security business units around the nation. It was then that he decided to start expanding his business acumen, including starting a seasoning distribution company (Opa Salt LLC) and writing this book. Among these activities, he is also working towards completion of the CISSP® certification, said to be the gold standard certification for cyber security professionals. When not engaging in his work-related activities, Skyler enjoys exercising, reading, traveling, smoking cigars, and spending time with friends and family.

Book Recommendations

As promised in Chapter 1, this is my list of further readings.

Don't Bullsh*t Yourself **by Jon Taffer** (Penguin, 2018)

This is a great book for identifying the excuses that you make in your life and how you can mitigate them to become the best version of yourself. This book gave me a mindset of "why not me?" when thinking about things I was hesitant about doing.

Getting from College to Career **(Rev. ed.) by Lindsey Pollak** (HarperBusiness, 2012)

While I hope that my book will cover what you need to help you get your two pieces of paper, it's never a bad idea to get a second opinion or perhaps more advice. This book should do that in a more "adult" way.

The Seven-Day Weekend **by Ricardo Semler** (Penguin, 2004)

This came as a recommendation from one of my managers during one of my internships. It's a bit longer read, but it's interesting from a historical perspective. It was first published in 2003, and some of the observations of Semler are readily seen in the modern working world now. My main takeaway was to be an adult and treat people like an adult.

Freakonomics by Steven D. Levitt and Stephen J. Dubner (Harper Perennial, 2009)

Life isn't fair, and *Freakonomics* shows quantitatively why that's the case. By taking an economical and analytical approach to the way the world works, it's easier to see how to get closer to prosperity. A really good and interesting read, and there's an ongoing podcast when you're finished.

Blink by Malcolm Gladwell (Little, Brown, 2007)

Blink is an important book because it unmasks how our optics trick us into believing things that are not true. I definitely believe that I am a less ignorant and more empathetic person having read this book.

End Notes

1   http://newsroom.ucla.edu/releases/heri-freshman-survey
    -242619

2   https://www.usnews.com/best-colleges/rankings/national
    -universities/freshmen-least-most-likely-return

3   https://www.collegeatlas.org/college-dropout.html

4   https://www.washingtonpost.com/business/2018/10/04/
    us-student-loan-debt-reaches-staggering-trillion/?utm_
    term=.e8e5c3e7b9b0

5   https://nces.ed.gov/fastfacts/display.asp?id=372

6   https://www.nerdwallet.com/blog/2018-fafsa-study

7   https://nces.ed.gov/pubs2018/2018434.pdf

8   https://hechingerreport.org/for-millions-of-college-dropouts
    -second-chances-prove-difficult

9   https://www.goodcall.com/news/how-much-more-can-you-make-with-a-masters-degree-01529

10 https://www.huffingtonpost.com/michaelprice/7-reasons-why-you-shouldn_1_b_5501111.html

11 https://www.youtube.com/watch?v=pw_9t82qD60

12 https://www.bls.gov/news.release/hsgec.nr0.htm

13 https://www2.deloitte.com/content/dam/Deloitte/global/Documents/About-Deloitte/gx-2018-millennial-survey-report.pdf

14 https://medium.com/@jchyip/why-t-shaped-people-e8706198e437

15 https://www.glassdoor.com/blog/scanning-resumes

16 https://hbswk.hbs.edu/item/minorities-who-whiten-job-resumes-get-more-interviews

17 https://www.statista.com/statistics/456500/daily-number-of-e-mails-worldwide

18 https://www.bbc.com/news/health-38896790

19 https://www.cnbc.com/2018/05/30/70-percent-of-people-globally-work-remotely-at-least-once-a-week-iwg-study.html

20 http://www.pewinternet.org/2018/03/01/social-media-use-in-2018

21 http://www.pewinternet.org/2018/03/01/social-media-use-in-2018

22 https://www.omnicoreagency.com/linkedin-statistics

23 https://www.deseretnews.com/article/900027934/casual-becoming-the-norm-in-workplace-dress-codes.html

24 https://www.thebalancecareers.com/what-is-business-attire-1918075

25 http://time.com/5342599/history-of-interns-internships

26 https://www.monster.com/career-advice/article/how-millennials-can-debunk-stereotypes-at-work

CPSIA information can be obtained
at www.ICGtesting.com
Printed in the USA
JSHW031554121020
8692JS00001B/36